DISCARDED

SLAVERY IN KENTUCKY

1792-1865

BY

IVAN E. McDOUGLE, Ph.D.

A Dissertation submitted to the Faculty of Clark University, Worcester, Massachusetts, in partial Fulfillment of the Requirements for the Degree of Doctor of Philosophy, and accepted on the Recommendation of George H. Blakeslee

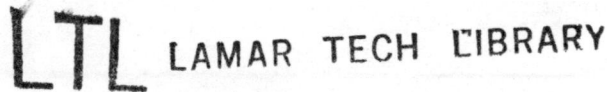

NEGRO UNIVERSITIES PRESS
WESTPORT, CONNECTICUT

Originally published in 1918
by the New Era Printing Company, Lancaster, Pa.

Reprinted 1970 by
Negro Universities Press
A DIVISION OF GREENWOOD PRESS, INC.
WESTPORT, CONN.

SBN 8371-3295-9

PRINTED IN UNITED STATES OF AMERICA

CONTENTS

Chapter	Page
1. Introduction	1
2. Development and General Status of Slavery	4
3. The Legal Status of Slavery	30
4. The Social Status of the Slave	71
5. Public Opinion regarding Emancipation and Colonization	93
Bibliography	119

SLAVERY IN KENTUCKY

CHAPTER I

INTRODUCTION

This study is an attempt to give a connected and concise account of the institution of slavery as it existed in the State of Kentucky from 1792 to 1865. Much has been written of slavery in other States, but there has not been published a single account which deals adequately with the institution in Kentucky. A scholarly treatise on *The Anti-Slavery Movement in Kentucky*, by Professor Asa E. Martin, of Pennsylvania State College, has appeared but, as this work is limited to a discussion of the history of the movement to overthrow slavery, our study parallels and supplements it.

In this study the chief emphasis has been placed upon the legal, economic and social history of slavery in Kentucky, mention being made of a few of the interesting anti-slavery incidents when these are known to have influenced the local status of the slave. We have first considered the inception of the system as based fundamentally upon the type of land settlement and tenure, followed by a study of the growth of the slave population, which brings in the question of the local economic value of the slave. An attempt has been made to explain the internal slave trade; and to consider to what extent Kentucky served as a breeding State for slaves destined to the market in the lower South.

In the chapter on the legal status of slavery special emphasis has been placed not only upon the legal position of the institution but upon the general evolution of the rights of the Negro in servitude. This section is vitally connected with the anti-slavery movement after about the year 1835. The problem of the fugitive slave and the general rights of emancipation and of the freed Negro have been approached purely from the legal standpoint.

The chapter on the social status of the slave considers the conditions of slave life that were more or less peculiar to Kentucky. There has often been made the statement, that in Kentucky Negro servitude was generally on a higher plane than in the States to the south and the treatment of slaves was much more humane. Some light has been thrown on these questions.

As a supplement to the discussion of the legal and social status a general summary of public opinion regarding emancipation and colonization has been added. Although for the most part consisting of previously published material this section has been treated from the viewpoint of the existing institution and not from the anti-slavery side which occasioned most of the original publication.

This study has been made from a consideration of the contemporary evidence as found in newspapers, statements of slaves, and general evidence of travelers and citizens of Kentucky during the period before the Civil War. The material for the study of this field is not only scattered throughout the country but for the most part it is very meager compared with the records of States like Virginia and Missouri. All the documents, papers, manuscripts and works known to be of value, however, have been consulted. The most valuable records for this treatise are to be found in the Durrett Collection at the University of Chicago, the extensive files of early Kentucky papers in the Library of the American Antiquarian Society, and the documents in the Kentucky State Library at Frankfort.

INTRODUCTION 3

To Mr. Clarence S. Brigham, of the American Antiquarian Society, Mr. Edward A. Henry, of the University of Chicago Library, and Mr. Frank Kavanaugh, of the Kentucky State Library, I am indebted for invaluable assistance rendered in securing material for this work. The treatment of the legal status of slavery would have been very meager, were it not for the valuable aid given by Dr. George E. Wire, of the Worcester County (Massachusetts) Law Library. To Miss Florence Dillard, of the Lexington (Kentucky) Public Library, I am indebted for assistance given throughout the period of my studies. To Prof. George H. Blakeslee, of Clark University, I owe more than to any one else—for his inspiration during my three years of study, for his most valuable aid in the correction of the manuscript, his candid judgment and judicial reasoning and the many suggestions which have helped to make this study what it is.

IVAN E. McDOUGLE

CLARK UNIVERSITY,
WORCESTER, MASSACHUSETTS.

CHAPTER II

THE DEVELOPMENT OF SLAVERY

It is impossible to understand slavery in Kentucky without some knowledge of the method by which the land was settled in the latter part of the eighteenth century. Between 1782 and 1802 the seven States which had interest in western lands ceded their rights to the United States and all that territory with the exception of Kentucky and the Connecticut Reserve in Ohio was made a part of the public domain. Hence, one of the distinguishing features of the settlement of Kentucky as compared with Ohio was that in the latter State the land was sold by the Federal Government to settlers coming from all parts of the country but particularly from the northeastern section. The result of this was that few citizens of Ohio held more than 640 acres.

Kentucky had been reserved by Virginia and consequently the method of settlement was purely a matter governed by that State and was separate and apart from the system which was employed by the United States Government. Furthermore, Kentucky lands were all given out by 1790, just one year after the beginning of our national period. The federal land policy was at that time just beginning. Virginia gave out the lands in Kentucky by what is known as the patent system, and all the settlers in Kentucky held their lands by one of three different kinds of rights.

In the first place there were those who were given tracts in the new territory as a reward for military services which had been rendered in the Revolution. This had been provided for by the legislature of Virginia as early as December, 1778.[1] No land north of the Ohio River was to be granted out as a military bounty until all the "good lands" in the

[1] Hening's Statutes, Vol. X, p. 50.

Kentucky region had been exhausted. The size of these tracts was to be governed by the official status of the recipient in the late war, and the bounties finally granted by Virginia ranged all the way from one hundred to fifteen thousand acres.²

The Virginia legislature of 1779 found it necessary to establish a second method of settlement in Kentucky in response to the demands of the large number of people who were migrating to the west of the Alleghenies. Provision was made for the granting of preemption rights to new settlers and also for the introduction of a very generous system of settlement rights. These settlement and preemption rights were almost inseparable, as the latter was dependent upon the former. It was provided that four hundred acres of land would be given to every person or family who had settled in the region before the first of January, 1778.³ The word "settlement" was stated to mean either a residence of one year in the territory or the raising of a crop of corn. In addition to the above grant every man who had built only a cabin or made any improvement on the land was entitled to a preemption of one thousand acres, providing such improvements had been made prior to January 1, 1778. Preference in the grants was to be given to the early settlers and even the most famous heroes of the Revolution were not allowed to interfere with the rights of those who held a certificate of settlement.

Thus far provision had been made only for those who had settled before 1778. To them was given the best of the land. Thereafter all settlement and preemption rights ceased and the further distribution of land in Kentucky was by means of treasury warrants. A person desiring land in Kentucky would appear at one of the Virginia land offices and make an entry and pay a fee amounting to about two cents per acre. The paper he would receive would give the approximate location of the tract and the recipient would

² Hening's Statutes, Vol. XI, p. 309; Treat, P. J., *National Land System*, p. 235.

³ *Ibid.*, Vol. X, pp. 35–45.

proceed to have the land surveyed at his pleasure. Within three months after the survey had been made he was to appear at the land office and have the same recorded. A copy of this record was to be taken to the assistant register of the land office in Kentucky and there it was to remain six months in order to give prior settlers, if any, the right to prove their claims to the property. No such evidence being produced a final record of the patent was to be made and a copy given to the original grantee.[4]

An interesting example of this method of settlement is shown by the experience of Abraham Lincoln, the grandfather of President Lincoln. On March 4, 1780, soon after the establishment of the new system, he appeared at the land office in Richmond, Virginia, and was given three treasury warrants, each for four hundred acres of land in Kentucky. The first and third of these warrants were not returned for the final recording until May 16, 1787, at which time Beverly Randolph, Governor of Virginia, issued a final deed of 800 acres of land in Lincoln County, Kentucky, to Abraham Lincoln.[5] The second treasury warrant was not returned until July 2, 1798, more than a decade after the death of Abraham Lincoln and six years after Kentucky had become a State. At that time the warrant was presented with a record of the survey by Mordecai Lincoln, the eldest son of Abraham. After some period of investigation the deed for the four hundred acres in Jefferson County was turned over to Mordecai Lincoln on April 26, 1799.[6]

The result of this method of granting land was that Kentucky was settled by a comparatively few men who rented their property to tenants. A large number of the military bounties were never settled by the original owners but were farmed by the later incoming tenant class. George Washington had been given five thousand acres and this land was actually settled by the poorer white element. In the

[4] Winterbotham, *An Historical Geographical Commercial and Topographical View of the United States*, Vol. 3, pp. 156–157.
[5] Kentucky Land Grants, Book 13, p. 59.
[6] *Ibid.*, Book 8, p. 228.

case of the land warrant property it was true that it was usually granted to the poorer class of early settlers but as in the instance of the Lincoln family the land soon passed into the hands of the wealthier settlers either by purchase or through law suits. It is commonly stated that Daniel Boone thus became landless and was forced to migrate to Missouri.[7]

Thus we see that Kentucky was distinctly different from all the other settlements to the west of the Alleghenies in the original system of land tenure and she further inherited from her mother State of Virginia the ancient theory of a landed aristocracy which was based upon tenantry. The early inhabitants of Kentucky can be easily divided into three classes, the landed proprietors, their slaves, and the tenant class of whites. The second and third classes tended to keep alive the status of the former and led to the perpetuation of the landed aristocracy. In Kentucky, however, the laws of descent were always against primogeniture and this resulted in the division of the lands of the wealthier class with each new generation.

The institution of slavery in Kentucky, as in every other State, depended for the most part upon the existence of large plantations. The only reason Kentucky had such large estates was because of the method by which the land was given out by the mother State. Economically Kentucky was not adapted to plantation life. The greater part of the State required then, as it still does, the personal care and supervision of the owner or tenant. The original distribution of land made this impossible and there grew up a large class of landholders who seldom labored with their hands, because of the traditional system. A large number of inhabitants as early as 1805, Michaux found, were cultivating their lands themselves, but those who could do so had all the work done by Negro slaves.[8]

With passing years, while Kentucky maintained slavery,

[7] Shaler's *Autobiography*, p. 33.
[8] Michaux (Thwaite's Reprint), *Travels to the West of the Allegheny Mountains*, Vol. 3, p. 237.

it came to have a social system not like that in the South but one more like the typical structure of the middle nineteenth century West. There were several reasons for this. In the first place, the absence of the policy of primogeniture in time came to distribute the lands over a much larger population. In the second place, while all the land in Kentucky had been granted by the year 1790, the patrician landholding element was completely submerged by the flood of so-called plebeians who came in soon after Kentucky became a State. In 1790 there were only 61,133 white people in Kentucky, and although all the land had been granted, the white population in the next decade nearly tripled, reaching 179,871 in 1800, and this increase, at a slightly smaller rate, continued down to about 1820. Still further the nature of the soil made it more profitable for the wealthier landed class to let out their holdings to the incoming whites who did their own work and in time came to own the property. "Each year increased this element of the state at the expense of the larger properties."[9]

A study of the growth of the slave and white population of Kentucky from 1790 to 1860 is necessary to an adequate understanding of the slave problem. It will be found ad-

POPULATION FROM 1790 TO 1860 WITH RATES OF INCREASE

	White	Per Cent Increase	Free Colored	Per Cent Increase	Slave	Per Cent Increase	Total	Per Cent Increase
1790..	61,133		114		11,830		73,077	
1800..	179,871	194.22	741	550.00	40,343	241.02	220,955	202.36
1810..	324,237	80.26	1,713	131.17	80,561	99.69	406,511	83.98
1820..	434,644	34.05	2,759	61.06	126,732	57.31	564,317[10]	38.82
1830..	517,787	19.12	4,917	78.21	165,213	30.36	687,917	21.09
1840..	590,253	13.99	7,317	48.81	182,258	10.31	779,828	13.36
1850..	761,413	28.99	10,011	36.81	210,981	15.75	982,405	25.98
1860..	919,484	20.76	10,684	6.72	225,483	6.87	1,155,684[11]	17.64

vantageous to deal with two sets of figures—one relating to the slave population within the State and the other with the slave increase in Kentucky as compared with the general

[9] Shaler, N. S., *Kentucky*, p. 196.
[10] Includes 182 Indians.
[11] Includes 33 Indians.

increase throughout the United States. It would not be of any value to compare the figures for Kentucky with those of any other State, for that would involve the discussion of local factors which are beyond the scope of this investigation.

First of all we shall take the census statistics for the State for all eight of the enumerations which were taken during the slavery era. The figures for the year 1790 were originally taken when Kentucky was a part of the State of Virginia, but they are included, since Kentucky became a State before the census was published. Furthermore they furnish an interesting light upon the growth of the slave population during the first decade of the new commonwealth. The important part of this table is in the increases, on a percentage basis, in the slave and white populations. Another viewpoint of the growth of the slave population may be seen in this little table:

RATIO OF SLAVES TO THE TOTAL POPULATION

	Per Cent		Per Cent
1790	16.1	1830	24.0
1800	18.2	1840	23.3
1810	19.18	1850	21.4
1820	22.4	1860	19.5

Here it will be seen that the proportion of slaves increased down to 1830 and then began to decline. Most authorities are agreed that this was in a large measure due to the enactment of the law of 1833 forbidding the importation of slaves

FREE NEGRO AND SLAVE POPULATION OF THE UNITED STATES, 1790 TO 1860, WITH RATES OF INCREASE

	Free Negro	Per Cent Increase	Slaves	Per Cent Increase
1790	59,557		697,624	
1800	108,435	82.1	893,602	28.1
1810	186,446	71.9	1,191,362	33.3
1820	233,634	25.3	1,538,022	29.1
1830	319,599	36.8	2,009,043	30.6
1840	386,293	20.9	2,487,355	23.8
1850	434,495	12.5	3,204,313	28.8
1860	488,070	12.3	3,953,760	23.4

into Kentucky. But before dealing with that question it would be well to have before us the figures for the whole country at the same period.

The facts seem more significant, if we compare the slave increase in Kentucky with that of the Negroes in the country as a whole. Bearing in mind that Kentucky was a comparatively new region when it became a State and that at that time slavery was firmly established along the seaboard, we are not surprised to find that the slave increase in Kentucky was much more rapid for the first three or four decades than it was in the nation as a whole. After the year 1830 the increase in the United States, on a percentage basis, was much greater than in Kentucky. It seems that the institution started in with a boom and then eventually died down in Kentucky.

There were several reasons for this fact. A glance at the increase of whites in Kentucky for the last three decades will show that they were forging ahead while the slaves were relatively declining. This was due to a large amount of immigration of that class of white people who were not slaveholding. A second factor was the non-importation act of 1833. About the same time there came to be a conviction among a large portion of the population that slavery in Kentucky was economically unprofitable. There is abundant ground for the position that the law of 1833 was passed because of a firm conviction that there were enough slaves in the State. The only ones who could profit by any amount of importation were the slave dealers and beyond a certain point even their trade would prove unprofitable. If there was ever a single slaveholder who defended importation on the ground that more slaves were needed in Kentucky he never spoke out in public and gave his reasons for such a position.

Unfortunately there are few statistics concerning the number of slaveholders in Kentucky. Cassius M. Clay in his appeal to the people in 1845 stated that there were 31,495 owners of slaves in the State.[12] The same year the

[12] Greeley, Horace, *Writings, Speeches and Addresses of Cassius M. Clay*, p. 177.

auditor's tax books showed that there were 176,107 slaves in Kentucky.[13] This would mean an average of 5.5 slaves for each owner. The accuracy of these figures is substantiated by those for the census of 1850 which gave 210,981 slaves held by 38,456 slaveholders or an average of 5.4 to each owner. These holders were classified according to the number of slaves held as follows:

```
Holders of 1 slave .............................. 9,244
Holders of over 1 and less than 5 slaves ......... 13,284
Holders of 5 and under 10 slaves ................ 9,579
Holders of 10 and under 20 slaves ............... 5,022
Holders of 20 and under 50 slaves ............... 1,198
Holders of 50 and under 100 slaves ..............    53
Holders of 100 and under 200 slaves .............     5
                                                 38,385[14]
```

This distribution shows that, although the average number of slaves held may have been 5.4 for each slaveholder, 21,528 or 50 per cent of them held less than five slaves each, and that 34,129 or 88 per cent held less than 20 each. Of the 132,920 free families in the State only 28 per cent held any slaves at all. This was somewhat below the average for the whole South. The total number of families holding slaves in the United States, by the census of 1850, was 347,525. With an average of 5.7 persons to each family there were about 2,000,000 persons in the relation of slave owners, or about one third of the whole white population of the slave States. In South Carolina, Alabama, Mississippi, and Louisiana about one half of the white population was thus classified. As stated above, this percentage in Kentucky was only twenty-eight.

This comparison can be more clearly shown by a table of the slave States from the census of 1850 showing the number of white people, the slaveholders, slaves, and the average number of slaves for each slaveholder.

[13] *Collected Documents*, 1847, p. 581.
[14] De Bow's *Statistical Review*, p. 95.

SLAVERY IN KENTUCKY

	Whites	Slave-holders	Per Cent of Whites	Slaves	Average per Holder
Alabama	426,514	29,295	6.8	342,844	11.6
Arkansas	162,189	5,999	3.7	47,100	7.8
Florida	47,203	3,520	7.4	39,310	11.1
Georgia	521,572	38,456	7.3	381,622	9.9
Kentucky	761,413	38,385	5.0	210,981	5.4
Louisiana	255,491	20,670	8.0	244,809	11.4
Maryland	417,943	16,040	3.8	90,368	5.6
Mississippi	295,718	23,116	7.8	309,878	13.4
Missouri	592,004	19,185	3.2	87,422	4.5
North Carolina	553,028	28,303	5.1	288,548	10.2
South Carolina	274,563	25,596	9.3	384,984	15.0
Tennessee	756,836	33,864	4.4	239,459	7.0
Texas	154,034	7,747	5.2	58,161	7.5
Virginia	894,800	55,063	6.1	472,528	8.5

Among the fourteen real slaveholding States of the Union Kentucky stood ninth in the number of slaves in 1850, but was third in the number of slave owners and with the exception of Missouri had less slaves for each owner than any other State. From the third column of this table, however, we are rather surprised to find that not only in Missouri but in Arkansas, Maryland and Tennessee the number of slaveholders was smaller in proportion to the total white population than in Kentucky.

Helper in his *Impending Crisis* made the following interesting table from the census figures for 1850. He set a perfectly arbitrary valuation of $400 on each slave, but, if

	Value of Slaves at $400 per Head	Value of Real and Personal Property Less the Value of Slaves
Alabama	$137,137,600	$ 81,066,732
Arkansas	18,840,000	21,001,025
Florida	15,724,000	7,474,734
Georgia	152,672,800	182,752,914
Kentucky	84,392,400	217,236,056
Louisiana	97,923,600	136,075,164
Maryland	36,147,200	183,070,164
Mississippi	123,951,200	105,000,000
Missouri	34,968,800	102,278,907
North Carolina	115,419,200	111,381,272
South Carolina	153,993,600	134,264,094
Tennessee	95,783,600	111,671,104
Texas	23,264,400	32,097,940
Virginia	189,011,200	202,634,638

[15] Adapted from De Bow's *Statistical Review*, pp. 67, 85, 99.

one takes into account the infants and the aged unable to work, his general appraisement of the slave group is fair enough for the time and for a basis of comparison. It will be seen at a glance that after taking out the value of the slaves in all the States Kentucky was the richest southern commonwealth.

From the three preceding tables it is apparent that while the Kentucky slaveholders represented about 28 per cent of the white population of the State, on the average they held less slaves than in the other Southern States. Slave property in Kentucky was a much smaller part of the wealth of the commonwealth than in the States to the south. The relatively large number of holders is to be explained by the type of slavery which existed in the State. Many persons held a few servants in bondage and those who held many slaves were very few in number.

The question of the sale of slaves from Kentucky into the southern market presents a much more formidable problem. The chief charge that the anti-slavery people made against Kentucky was that the State regularly bred and reared slaves for the market in the lower South. What was the attitude of the Kentucky slaveholder and the people in general on the question of the domestic slave trade? There is no doubt that in the later years of slavery there were sold in the State many slaves who ultimately found their way into the southern market notwithstanding the contempt of the average Kentucky slaveholder for the slave trade. This trend of opinion will be seen as we proceed. If the sentiment was decidedly against such human commerce how did so many slaves become victims of the slave trader?

There were five general causes which led to the sale of slaves in Kentucky: (1) When they became so unruly that the master was forced to sell; (2) when their sale was necessary to settle an estate; (3) when the master was reduced to the need of the money value in preference to the labor; (4) when captured runaways were unclaimed after one year; and (5) when the profit alone was desired by unscrupulous masters. Many other reasons have been given, but a careful investigation of all available material confines practically every known case of sale to one of the above classifications. Mrs. Stowe in her *Key to Uncle Tom's Cabin*[16] maintained that the prevalence of the slave trade in Kentucky was due to the impoverishment of the soil beyond recovery and the decrease in the economic value of the slave to its owner. This argument is fallacious, for the very blue-grass region which held most of the slaves is today the most fertile section of the State.

As long as a slave conducted himself in accordance with the spirit of the slave code there was little chance of his owner selling him against his will. The president of the Constitutional Convention of 1849 stated that in the interior of the State, where slaves were the most numerous, very few Negroes were sold out of the State and that they were mostly those whose bad and ungovernable disposition was such that their owners could no longer control them.[17] A true picture of the average master's attitude has been given us by Prof. N. S. Shaler. "What negroes there were," said he, "belonged to a good class. The greater number of them were from families which had been owned by the ancestors of their masters in Virginia. In my grandfather's household and those of his children there were some two dozen of these blacks. They were well cared for; none of them were ever sold, though there was the common threat that 'if you don't behave, you will be sold South.' One of the commonest bits of instruction my grandfather gave me was to remember that my people had in a century never bought or sold a slave except to keep families together. By that he meant that a gentleman of his station should not run any risk of appearing as a 'negro trader,' the last word of opprobrium to be slung at a man. So far as I can remember, this rule was well kept and social ostracism was likely to be visited on any one who was fairly suspected of buying or selling slaves for profit. This state of opinion was, I believe, very general among the better class of slave

[16] Stowe, *Key to Uncle Tom's Cabin*, p. 143.
[17] *Louisville Weekly Journal*, October 17, 1849.

owners in Kentucky. When negroes were sold it was because they were vicious and intractable. Yet there were exceptions to this high-minded humor."[18]

When a master had a bad Negro about the only thing that could be done for the sake of discipline was to sell him. If the owner kept the slave, the latter would corrupt his fellows and if he were set free, the master would reward where he ought to punish. The human interest which the owner took in his servant when the demands of the institution necessitated his sale is shown in the case of the Negro Frank, owned by A. Barnett, of Greensburg. Witness these words of the master in a runaway advertisement: "His transgressions impelled me, some years since to take him to New Orleans and sell him, where he became the property of a Spaniard, who branded him on each cheek thus, ⊡, which is plain to be seen when said negro is newly shaved. I went to New Orleans again last May, where, having my feelings excited by the tale Frank told me, I purchased him again."[19] After the master had gone to all this trouble in the interest of the slave the latter ran away shortly after his return to Kentucky.

It was often necessary to sell slaves in order to settle an estate. It was seldom possible for a man to will his property in Negroes without some divisions becoming necessary at the hands of the executor in the just interest of the heirs. These public auctions usually took place on court day, at the courthouse door and were conducted by the master comsioner of the circuit court. The following advertisement reveals the necessity and the procedure:

SALE OF NEGROES

By virtue of a decree of the Fayette Circuit, the undersigned will, as Commissioner to carry into effect said decree, sell to the highest bidder, on the public square in the city of Lexington, on Monday the 10th of March next, being county court day, the following slaves, to wit:

[18] Shaler's *Autobiography*, p. 36.
[19] *Louisville Public Advertiser*, December 24, 1829.

Keiser, Carr, Sally, Bob, Susan, Sam, Sarah and Ben; belonging to the estate of Alexander Culbertson, deceased. The sale to be on a credit of three months, the purchaser to give bond with approved security. The sale to take place between the hours of 11 o'clock in the morning and 3 o'clock in the evening.

February 26, 1834   JOHN CLARK, *Commissioner*[20]

On the same day the sheriff of the county might appear at the courthouse door in accordance with a previous announcement and auction off any unclaimed runaway that had been lodged in the county jail or hired out under his authority for a period of a year or more. The slaves thus sold were usually fugitives from the lower South who had been apprehended on their way to Ohio or Indiana. Although the utmost publicity would have been given to their capture, in accordance with the law, few of the planters of the far South seem ever to have claimed their property. The usual legal code in this matter is shown by the notice below:

NOTICE: Agreeably to an act of the General Assembly, passed January 11, 1845, I will, on the first Monday of May, 1846, before the Court House door, in the city of Louisville, sell to the highest bidder, on a credit of six months, the purchaser giving bond with good security, having the force and effect of a replevin bond, JOHN, a runaway slave, 18 or 19 years of age, 5 feet 3 or 4 inches high, a rather heavy built, supposed to be the property of Daniel McCaleb or Calip, residing on the coast some twenty miles below New Orleans.

Feb. 25, 1846.   F. S. J. RONALD *Deputy Sheriff* for JAMES HARRISON *Sheriff Jefferson Co.*[21]

Under the three causes of sale thus far cited the blame would not be placed upon the master. In the case of the unruly Negro the owner was according to the ethics of that day not at fault. In the settlement of an estate the slaveholder was no longer a factor, for his demise alone had

[20] *Lexington Observer* and *Kentucky Reporter*, February 27, 1834.
[21] *Louisville Weekly Journal*, March 4, 1846.

brought the sale. In the case of the runaway the owner was unknown. Mrs. Stowe probably showed the attitude of the average Kentucky master when she pictured Uncle Tom as being sold for the southern market only because of the economic necessities of the owner. When in such a position the master felt called upon to explain the necessities of the case. He was very careful not to be cast under the suspicion of public opinion as a "slave trader," which, as Shaler has said, was the "last word of opprobrium." Witness a few instances in evidence:

NEGROES FOR SALE

A yellow negro woman of fine constitution, and two children, from the country, and sold for no fault but to raise money. Will not be sold to go down the river. Her husband, a fine man, can be had also. Apply at the store of

JARVIS AND TRABUE—3rd & Main[22]

The editor of the *Lexington Reporter* was very careful not to get under the ban of his constituents when he was forced to sell a farm hand and his wife.

FOR SALE

A negro man, a first rate farm hand, about 27 years of age; and a very likely woman, the wife of the man, about 22 years of age, a good house servant. They will not be sold separately, or to any person wishing to take them out of the State. Enquire at this office.[23]

In 1834 Thomas J. Allen, a citizen of Louisville, desired to exchange his property in the city for 40 or 50 slaves, but he specifically stated that they were to be for his own use and that he wanted them to be "in families."[24] The same attitude appears in the case of a house servant for sale with the reasons for such specifically stated:

[22] *Louisville Weekly Journal*, September 3, 1845.
[23] *Lexington Observer* and *Kentucky Reporter*, Jan. 28, 1835.
[24] *Ibid.*, July 9, 1834.

FOR SALE

I wish to sell a negro woman, who has been accustomed to house work. She is an excellent cook, washes and scours, and is in every respect, an active and intelligent servant. I do not require her services, which is my only reason for wishing to dispose of her.

Maslin Smith[25]

The prevalence of statements giving the reasons for and the restrictions upon these sales should show beyond any reasonable doubt that public opinion would not tolerate any suspicion of a heartless traffic in slaves. These sentiments were especially prevalent in the central portion of the State. The only case known to the writer where a large number of slaves were sold without any qualification was near Harrodsburg in August, 1845; but in this instance all the man's property, including 450 acres of land, was sold at the same time.[26]

There were, naturally, some unscrupulous masters who cared little for the fate of their slaves when sold. They placed no restrictions upon the sale, either in destination or in the break-up of family ties. We will cite only two, one for the earlier and one for the later period, noticeable chiefly for the lack of regard for Negro family life.

NEGROES FOR SALE

The subscriber has for sale a negro man and woman, each about 24 years of age, both are excellent plantation hands, together with two children. They will be sold separately or altogether.

Luidores Lucas[27]

.FOR SALE

I wish to sell a negro woman and four children. The woman is 22 years old, of good character, a good cook and washer. The children are very likely, from 6 years down to 1½. I will sell them together or separately to suit purchasers.

J. T. Underwood.[28]

---

[25] *Lexington Observer* and *Kentucky Reporter*, Jan. 7, 1835.
[26] *Louisville Weekly Journal*, August 6, 1845.
[27] *Bairdstown Candid Review*, June 20, 1809.
[28] *Louisville Weekly Journal*, May 2, 1849.

The aggregate of all these causes was sufficient to bring about a supply for the southern market. The question now arises as to how the demand was met commercially. To what extent were there slave traders in Kentucky? George Prentice, the famous editor of the *Louisville Journal,* himself a loyal exponent of slavery, early pointed out that Kentucky had an ample supply of Negroes and that they were being sent south in large numbers. He further stated that any one who wanted slaves could always purchase them by leaving an order in Louisville.[29] This opinion was expressed at a time when the non-importation act of 1833 had been in force for sixteen years, which meant that Kentucky was producing slaves faster than she needed them. It was only two months after this that Richard Henry Collins in an editorial in the *Maysville Eagle* gave a flagrant example of a slave trader in Kentucky who violated the spirit as well as the letter of the law. But the sentiment of the people on the slave dealer had been expressed much earlier. In 1833 a Lexington editor felt exasperated because of the appearance of a large group of slaves in the streets of the city on their way to be sold south. When another trader appeared with his Negro slaves held together with a chain he voiced his wrath in this fashion:

"A few weeks ago we gave an account of a company of men, women and children, part of them manacled, passing through the streets. Last week, a number of slaves were driven through the main street of our city, among them were a number manacled together, two abreast, all connected by, and supporting, a heavy iron chain, which extended the whole length of the line."[30]

About the same time a citizen of Danville sold a Negro woman to a regular slave trader. The news spread around the town rapidly and to save himself from the threats of the gathering mob the owner was compelled for his own safety to follow the slave dealer and repurchase the woman at a decided increase in price.[31]

[29] *Louisville Weekly Journal,* September 26, 1849.
[30] *Lexington Western Luminary,* June 5, 1833.
[31] Blanchard and Rice, *Debates on Slavery,* p. 133.

It is very difficult to find out how many slave dealers there were in the State, for few of them ever came out in the open and advertised their trade. As would be expected from its size and situation Louisville was the place where the dealer could ply his trade to the best advantage. It was the central business point and the port from which most slaves from Kentucky were shipped down the Ohio and Mississippi. There is no mention in the newspapers of any dealers there before the year 1845. Thereafter there were several who advertised for any number of slaves and made no secret of the purpose of purchase. In the *Journal* for October 29, 1845, William Kelly called for all persons who had slaves to sell to see him and offered them the highest prices. He further stated that he had slaves for sale. His name does not often appear in succeeding years. During the next decade there were four regular dealers who apparently did considerable business: T. Arterburn, J. Arterburn, William F. Talbott, and Thomas Powell. Later John Mattingly came upon the scene presumably from St. Louis. In July, 1845, the Arterburn brothers began a series of advertisements which ran for several years. "We wish to purchase 100 negroes for the Southern market, for which we will pay the highest prices in cash."[32] Talbott began his publicity in 1848 with these words: "The subscriber wishes to purchase 100 negroes, for which he will pay the highest cash prices. Can always be found at the Louisville Hotel."[33] Two years later he was still advertising, but had ceased placing any limit on the number to be bought and had moved his quarters to the Hotel O'Rain.[34] Thomas Powell also began in 1848 with this stock phraseology— "Persons having negroes for sale can find a purchaser at the highest cash prices by calling on the subscriber, on Sixth Street, between Main and Market, adjoining H. Duncan's stable."[35] This advertisement ran continually for a period

[32] *Louisville Weekly Journal*, July 30, 1845.
[33] *Ibid.*, July 19, 1848.
[34] *Ibid.*, August 14, 1850.
[35] *Ibid.*, August 2, 1848.

of two years. John Mattingly evidently came from Missouri in the same year, and remained until 1852, when he returned to St. Louis to ply his trade.[36] While he was in Louisville he ran an advertisement in the *Journal* after this fashion: "The undersigned wishes to purchase 100 negroes both men and women, for which he will pay the highest cash prices. Those who have negroes for sale would do well to call on him at the Galt House."[37]

It is noticeable that none of the Louisville directories for this period mention any slave dealers. This failure may have been due merely to the fact that there were so few traders in the city and that they were more or less transient residents. On the other hand, public opinion apparently never acknowledged that there were any real citizens of the city engaged in the slave trade. Beginning in 1840 the *Louisville Journal* published a weekly paper called *Louisville Prices Current*. In 1855 this was succeeded by the *Commercial Review and Louisville Prices Current*, which was published by the Louisville Chamber of Commerce. These two papers devoted themselves exclusively to the commercial transactions of the city and gave price quotations weekly for every conceivable kind of goods in the market together with the volume of sales. Strange to say, there has not been found a single issue of either of these papers, which mentions the selling price of slaves or any transaction in Negroes. If there was a trade in slaves which was regarded purely as a commercial enterprise, as some would have us think, then it is very hard to understand why these splendid trade papers did not contain any account of the business.

There were some Louisville business men who bought and sold slaves as only one of the branches of their commercial activities. This would account to some extent for the failure to list traders in the local directories for it is noticeable that such men never called themselves slave dealers. As early as the year 1825 John Stickney estab-

[36] *St. Louis Daily Times,* October 14, 1852.
[37] *Louisville Daily Journal,* November 23, 1848.

lished the *Louisville Intelligence Office* on Main Street, which was a sort of labor and real estate exchange. He advertised that he sold books; had money to loan; houses for rent and sale; horses and Negroes for sale and hire; carriages for sale; conducted a labor exchange, and recommended the best boarding houses.[38] A year later J. C. Gentry opened the "Western Horse Market" at the corner of Market and Fourth Streets. He advertised that he conducted a livery stable, and also sold on commission, at public or private sale, horses, carriages, cattle, wagons and slaves; and that he would conduct an auction on Wednesdays and Saturdays.[39] A similar case was that of A. C. Scott, who in 1854 opened a real estate and land office but who stated in the press that he not only bought and sold land and rented houses but that he would sell and hire slaves.[40] Consequently Scott was listed as a real estate and land agent in the local directories. It is impossible to determine how many of these occasional slave dealers there were, but in so far as available material shows these three were the only ones to announce their trade publicly.

It would appear from all the evidence at hand that while Kentucky furnished many slaves for the southern market there was no general internal slave trade, as a commercial enterprise. There were in Louisville, however, a few heartless business men who took advantage of the decreasing value of slave labor in Kentucky and the rising prices of slaves in the far South. In this respect, Kentucky became a field of supply for the slave markets of the lower South.

Unfortunately there are no statistics available by which the number of slaves sent south can be computed. The most comprehensive anti-slavery publication on the internal slave trade was unable to decide with certainty what proportion of slaves for the southern market was furnished by each of the so-called breeding States. The author of *Slavery and Internal Slave Trade in the United States*

[38] *Louisville Public Advertiser*, November 2, 1825.
[39] *Ibid.*, September 13, 1826.
[40] *Louisville Daily Times*, March 1, 1854.

The Development of Slavery

estimated that 80,000 slaves were annually exported from seven States to the South. He gave no figures that were not his own estimates. He ranked the seven States, however, in the order of the number of slaves which he thought they furnished as follows: Virginia, Maryland, North Carolina, Kentucky, Tennessee, Missouri and Delaware.[41]

Martin estimates that Kentucky sent on the average about 5,000 slaves to the southern market.[42] Again this must be considered purely conjectural. It is reasonable to suppose that during the last two decades of the slavery era there were few slaves imported into Kentucky that were intended for the purely Kentucky market. What Negroes came into Kentucky were for the most part on their way to the more profitable southern trade. The average death rate among the slaves during this period was 1.9 per one hundred and the birth rate was 3.2, or an excess of births over deaths of 1.1 per hundred. This would make the annual natural increase among the slave population about 2,000 per year. Comparing this with the growth of the slave group from 1840 to 1850 we find that the increase of slaves was much more. But it was during the next decade that the slave trade reached its height and here we find that the slave population increased 14,502, whereas the natural increase during that period should have been 23,190. Hence the slaves failed to reach even their natural increase by a deficiency of 8,688. Taken literally that would mean that during the ten-year period that number of slaves were exported from Kentucky. But it is reasonable to suppose that many more than that were sent to the South. With the exception of the last decade, however, the slave population of Kentucky increased faster than the mere natural increase of the Negroes. The law would not permit of any importation of slaves intended for Kentucky, so the export of purely Kentucky slaves appears never to have been prominent except during the decade from 1850 to 1860.

The selling price of slaves naturally presents itself at

[41] *Slavery and Internal Slave Trade in the U. S.*, p. 12.
[42] Martin, Asa E., *Anti-Slavery Movement in Kentucky*, p. 89.

this point. In Kentucky these records are very few because the tax books in practically all the counties of the State have been destroyed. We have no accurate statements extant before about the year 1855. The prices which we have obtained are quotations from the auction of slaves of estates to settle the interests of the heirs. On January court day, in 1855, there were sold in the settlement of estates in Bourbon, Fayette, Clark and Franklin Counties Negro men who brought $1,260, $1,175, $1,070, $1,378, $1,295, $1,015 and $1,505.[43] The county commissioner of Harrison auctioned the slaves of the deceased George Kirkpatrick with the following prices received:

America	40 years of age	
Peggy	6 years of age	all for $1,600
Eliza	4 years of age	
Brown	6 months of age	
Peter	23 years of age	$1,290
Emanuel	24 years of age	750
Tom	16 years of age	1,015
Ann	14 years of age	775
Emma	12 years of age	865
Sarah	26 years of age	350[44]

The county commissioner at Henderson received the following prices for slaves in the settlement of several estates on January 28, 1858:[45]

Ruth	33 years of age	$ 800
Willis	59 years of age	475
George	35 years of age	1,200
Delphy	80 years of age	75
Leila	65 years of age	282
Clarissa	24 years of age	1,131
Andrew	19 years of age	1,500
Susan	17 years of age	470
Jennie	17 years of age	1,100
Cupid	85 years of age	74
Eliza	32 years of age	500
Bell	41 years of age	1,000

[43] Collins, *History of Kentucky*, Vol. 1, p. 74.
[44] *Cynthiana News*, January 10, 1858.
[45] *Henderson Weekly Commercial*, January 29, 1858.

The Development of Slavery 25

This sale is most significant for the cases of "Delphy," 80 years old, and "Cupid," 85 years of age. It is difficult to account for such a sale in any discussion of the slave trade, but it does show the humanitarian side of Kentucky slavery. Negroes at such an age had no economic value even if they were given away, because the expense of their maintenance was more than the value of any possible labor they could perform.

At Georgetown in December of the same year we have this record:[46]

Griffin	45 years of age	$ 640
Mary	14 years of age	1,060
Ellen	12 years of age	800
Elizabeth	11 years of age	406 (one-eyed)
Sanford	9 years of age	700
Arabel	10 years of age	690
Adam	41 years of age	700
Bettie	3 years of age	260
Aaron	28 years of age	1,191
Sam	25 years of age	1,350

The auction of the slaves of the estate of Spencer C. Graves at Lexington in April, 1859, brought these prices:[47]

John	18 years of age	$1,500
Dick	21 years of age	1,400
Jerry	38 years of age	700
Major	50 years of age	480
Charles	31 years of age	1,155
John Jr.	18 years of age	1,140
Billy	31 years of age	1,100
Isabella	40 years, with 3 children, ages 11, 5 and 2	1,610
Rebecca	30 years, with 3 children, ages 11, 6 and 4	2,410
Lucy	18 years of age, with infant	1,280
Davidella	31 years of age	1,220
Mary Ann	31 years of age	835
Patience	18 years of age	1,350
Catharine	15 years of age	1,130

Such a series of prices would show beyond a reasonable

[46] *Georgetown Gazette*, December 23, 1858.
[47] *Weekly Free South* (Newport), April 29, 1859.

doubt that the value of slaves was determined entirely by the increasing demand for slaves in the lower South and was in no way an indication of the value of slave labor within Kentucky. As was pointed out earlier in this chapter, the labor value of an agricultural slave in the State steadily decreased after about the year 1830.

Was slavery profitable to the Kentucky planters? In the many debates on the slavery question which took place after 1830 no one ever stood out in the affirmative. The only ones to discuss the economic side of the issue were those in opposition to slavery. As has often been said of the Kentucky situation, "the program was to use negroes to raise corn to feed hogs to feed negroes, who raised more corn to feed more hogs." Tobacco was the largest crop raised in the State and corn came next. Neither proved to be peculiarly adapted to slave labor. There were few large plantations in the State where it could be made advantageous. What Negro work there was to be done was never confined to any particular kind of cultivation but was used in the manner of farm labor today in the State. Squire Turner, of Madison County, in the Constitutional Convention of 1849 made a careful summary of the existing economic problems of slavery. "There are," said he, "about $61,000,000 worth of slave property in the state which produces less than three per cent profit on the capital invested, or about half as much as the moneyed capital would yield. There are about 200,000 slaves in Kentucky. Of these about seventy-five per cent are superannuated, sick, women in unfit condition for labor, and infants unable to work, who yield no profit. Show me a man that has forty or fifty slaves on his estate, and if there are ten out of that number who are available and valuable, it is as much as you can expect. But my calculation allows you to have seventy-five per cent who are barely able to maintain themselves, to pay for their own clothing, fuel, house room and doctor's bills. Is there any gentleman who has a large number of slaves, who will say that they are any more profitable than that?"[48]

[48] Debates of the Convention of 1849, p. 73.

No one in the convention answered the last question put by Squire Turner. But regardless of such an economic condition, not a single piece of remedial legislation was passed and the members of the Constitutional Convention added a provision to the Bill of Rights which rooted the slavery system firmer than ever. That most admirable of all southern characters, and at the same time the most difficult to understand, the Kentucky master, took little heed of a question of dollars and cents when it interfered with his moral and humanitarian sentiments. He had inherited, in most cases, the slaves that were his. He knew well enough that the system did not pay but supposing that he should turn his slaves loose, what would become of them? What could they do for a living? The experience of later years proved that his apparently obstinate temperament was mixed with a good deal of wisdom, for once the slaves were set free their status was not to any great extent ameliorated if they went abroad from the plantation where they had lived from childhood.

There was a certain amount of profit in the labor of able-bodied slaves but they only represented a fraction of the Negroes whom the master was called upon to support. The law compelled the owner to maintain his old and helpless slaves and this represented the spirit of the large majority of the slaveholders. Those were rare cases indeed when an owner was hailed into court for failing to provide for an infirm member of his slave household. The true Kentuckian never begrudged the expense that such support incurred. One of the ablest lawyers of the State, Benjamin Hardin, made the statement that "if it were not for supporting my slaves, I would never go near a courthouse."[49]

Rev. Stuart Robinson, speaking before the Kentucky Colonization Society in 1849, gave another viewpoint of the economic value of the slave. "The increase of slaves in Kentucky," said he, "has hardly reached three thousand annually for eighteen years past. The increase since 1840 has been 27,653—the increase for the year just closed 2,921.

[49] Little, L. P., *Ben Hardin, his Times and Contemporaries*, p. 544.

In twenty-six counties, embracing one fourth of the slave population—some of them the largest slave-holding counties—there has been an actual decrease in the last year of 881 slaves. In twelve other counties the increase has been only twenty-three. There are ten counties in the State, which contain one third of all the slave population of Kentucky; in these ten counties, the increase of slaves for five years past has been 2,728—an increase of less than one per cent per annum. Nor is this slow increase of slavery to be attributed to any stagnation or decline of public prosperity, for in the meantime the state has been growing in population and wealth as heretofore. During these five years the taxable property of the Commonwealth has increased in value more than seventy-six millions. Now this decrease of slaves while the other property of the commonwealth is increasing must arise from one of three causes— and in either case the inference is the same as to the fate of slavery in Kentucky. (1) Is it because the climate is unhealthy to the African? If so then African labor cannot continue. (2) Is it owing to emigration? Then something is wrong in the system of labor, that causes the emigration of our people—for no finer soil—no more desirable residence can be found in the world. (3) Or is it owing to the domestic slave trade? Then for some reason slave labor is less profitable here than elsewhere, and must soon be given up.''[50]

These figures quoted by the speaker on the slave population for year by year are available in the auditor's tax books for the years 1840 to 1859:[51]

1840	164,817	1847	189,549	1854	200,181
1841	168,853	1848	192,470	1855	202,790
1842	171,035	1849	195,110	1856	201,160
1843	176,107	1850	196,847	1857	201,590
1844	178,837	1851	196,336	1858	207,559
1845	182,742	1852	200,867	1859	208,625
1846	185,582	1853	200,015		

[50] *Presbyterian Herald*, April 12, 1849.
[51] *Collected Documents*, 1847, pp. 581–583; 1853, pp. 401–403; 1860, pp. 241–246.

The very small growth shown here would barely account for the natural increase among the slaves by virtue of the high birth rate. The mortality rates were about the same for slaves as for whites. The relative decline was undoubtedly due to the rising prices for slaves which were sent to the South and the consequent decreasing value of a slave's labor to the Kentuckian. He knew beyond a doubt that the time would eventually come when he would have to part with his slave and that portion of the holders who were not averse to selling their chattels did so during this period.

CHAPTER III

THE LEGAL STATUS OF SLAVERY

Slavery in its more economic form naturally spread to the Kentucky district as the western frontier of Virginia became settled. Of the 293,427 slaves which were held in the State of Virginia in the year 1790, however, only 11,830 were in the district of Kentucky, which at that time had a total population of 73,077. Few thought, however, of disputing the rights of the institution in the newly created State. The final convention which met to form a constitution was held at Danville, beginning on April 2, 1792, and in the course of its proceedings it was apparent that there was no fundamental division among the delegates regarding any of the proposed provisions with the exception of the one dealing with slavery. Virginia had stipulated in giving permission for the formation of the new State that slavery as an established institution should not be disturbed, and this policy had the support of a majority of the members of the constitutional convention. George Nichols, a native of the Old Dominion, was the leader of the assembly and had charge of most of tne work which was done and naturally was most interested in carrying out the wishes of his native State in the formation of the new document. The only serious opponent was David Rice, a noted Presbyterian minister, but, having resigned on April 11, he was not present at the time when the slavery issue came up for final settlement.

A separate vote was taken on Article IX, the slavery section, which passed 26 to 19. It was finally provided that

> The legislature shall have no power to pass laws for the emancipation of slaves without the consent of their owners, or without paying their owners, previous to such emancipation, a full equivalent in money, for the slaves emancipated; they shall have no power

to prevent immigrants to this state, from bringing with them such persons as are deemed slaves by the laws of any one of the United States, so long as any person of the same age or description shall be continued in slavery by the laws of this state: that they shall pass laws to permit the owners of slaves to emancipate them, saving the rights of creditors, and preventing them from becoming a charge to the county in which they reside; they shall have full power to prevent slaves from being brought into this state as merchandise; they shall have full power to prevent any slave being brought into this state from a foreign country, and to prevent those from being brought into this state, who have been since the first of January, 1789, or may hereafter be imported into any of the United States from a foreign country. And they shall have full power to pass such laws as may be necessary to oblige the owners of slaves to treat them with humanity, to provide for them necessary clothes and provisions, to abstain from all injuries to them extending to life or limb, and in case of their neglect or refusal to comply with the directions of such laws, to have such slave or slaves sold for the benefit of their owner or owners.[1]

In any discussion of the slavery question in Kentucky in its historical aspects this article of the first constitution is fundamental. It is evident that even at that early day the difficulty of the slavery problem was already in the minds of the people in spite of many other apparently more pressing issues. The article itself remained practically intact throughout the existence of slavery in the State. Were there ever in later years gathered within the confines of the State any body of men who had a better grasp of the future? The single instance of the recommendation that the legislature should pass laws permitting the emancipation of slaves only under the provision that they should be guaranteed from becoming a public charge to the county shows the comprehension of a difficulty that could not at such an early date have developed to any great degree, but which in later decades was a formidable problem. We may well say with John Mason Brown, however, that "the system of slavery thus contemplated was designed to be as

[1] *Littell's Laws*, 1: 32.

mild, as human, and as much protected from traffic evils as possible, but it was to be emphatically perpetual, for no emancipation could be had without the assent of each particular owner of each individual slave."[2]

The session of the State assembly which met in November, 1792, only attempted to carry out the constitutional provision prohibiting commercial transactions with slaves. No person was permitted to buy of, or sell to, any slave, any manner of thing whatsoever without a written permit descriptive of the article under the penalty of four times the value of the thing bought or sold. The jurisdiction of such cases was given to the county court, if they concerned values of more than five pounds. The slave was to receive ten lashes, which by the standards of those days was a meager punishment for any offense.[3] Whenever possible the slave was not brought into consideration as an offender. The theory seems to have been that the slave was better off when left alone. It was only when some unscrupulous outsider came in to use the slave either as a victim or as an object of profit that it was necessary to draw the strings tighter on the Negro, not because of any inherent tendency to crime so much as to keep the slave from becoming unruly when in the power of a superior influence.

It was not until the session of 1798 that the legislature drew up the fundamental slave code which was to carry out all the recommendations of the constitutional convention and which remained the basis of all legal action throughout the entire period of slavery. Among the early acts of the State had been the temporary adoption of the statutes of Virginia on the treatment of slaves and slavery problems, which were then in force.[4] These remained as a slave code for Kentucky until the enactment in 1798 of these new laws, which contained forty-three articles and involved almost every question that could come up for legal consideration in connection with the institution. The experience of six

[2] Brown, John Mason, *The Political Beginnings of Kentucky*, p. 229.
[3] *Littell's Laws*, 1: 44.
[4] *Ibid.*, 1: 161.

years as a separate State had served to show that many existing provisions of the Virginia code were not readily adapted to the rapidly growing State, and then too there was a decided tendency to ameliorate the condition of the slave as much as possible. In Kentucky they were not then, at least, confronted with such a large mass of slaves that they could not meet problems in a much easier manner than in the Old Dominion.

In the beginning, it was naturally found necessary to place some restrictions on the slave and his movements. He was not allowed to leave his master's plantation without written permission and if he did go away, any person could apprehend the offender and take him before a justice of the peace, who was empowered to order the infliction of stripes at his discretion. Furthermore, he was not to wander off to any other plantation without the written permission of his owner, with the provision in this instance that he was not to be taken before a justice of the peace, but before his owner, who was entitled to inflict ten lashes upon the offender. Should the slave be found carrying any powder, shot, a gun, club, or any weapon he could be apprehended by any free person and taken before a justice and a much severer penalty exacted in the form of thirty-nine lashes, "well laid on, on the bare back."[5] It is clear that this law was drawn up to keep the slave from becoming a public menace and not as a sign of absolute restriction on the servant, for it was further provided in Section 6 that in case the slave lived in a frontier community he could go to the local justice of the peace and secure a permit to keep and use guns, powder, shot and other weapons for either offensive or defensive purposes. This permission was to be indorsed by any free Negro, mulatto or Indian and did not necessarily involve the approval of the owner of the slave.

It was declared unlawful for slaves to engage in riots, unlawful assemblies, in trespasses or in seditious speech and, if so accused, they were to be taken before the local justice

[5] *Littell's Laws*, 2: 113.

who was to punish them at his discretion. But the Negroes themselves were not to be considered as the only guilty ones. In order to prevent any such disorderly meetings no owner of slaves was to be allowed to permit any slave not belonging to him to remain on his plantation for more than four hours at any one time under a nominal penalty to such owner of $2; but, if he allowed more than five such slaves to assemble on his property, he was to be fined more severely. If such a group were brought together by the written permission of the owner and for business reasons, however, there was involved no offense whatever.[6] It was realized that oftentimes the chief leaders in the unlawful meetings of slaves were free Negroes and sympathetic whites. Were any such to be found present they were to be arrested and if found guilty when tried before a justice of the peace, should be fined 15 shillings, to be paid, not to the court, but to the informer and if the money was not forthcoming the court was to have twenty lashes inflicted—no matter whether the convicted be white or black. Inasmuch as the degree of punishment of the slaves for being present at such a meeting was not specified it would seem that the legislature meant that the free persons involved should be treated more severely than slaves by the court.

The law of 1792 regarding trading with slaves had not proved to be effective, for in many cases the owner for a stipulated wage paid by the slave had permitted him to go at large and engage in trade as if he were a free man. The legislature found that this encouraged the slaves to commit thefts and engage in various evil practices and naturally censured the owner. A fine of $50 was to be paid by the master for each offending slave and no punishment whatever was to be given the latter. But should the servant go so far as to hire himself out, he would be imprisoned by order of the court and, at the next session of the county court, he would be sold. One fourth of the money thus received was to be applied to the county funds and 5 per cent was to be given to the sheriff and the owner was to

[6] *Littell's Laws*, 2: 114.

receive the remaining 70 per cent. Here too the slave was not punished and his condition of servitude was not changed. It was merely a change of owners. Again the offending owner was the victim and for his carelessness he was deprived of 30 per cent of the money value of his slave.[7]

The leading Kentucky case bearing on slaves engaged in trade is that of Bryant *vs.* Sheely (5 Dana, 530). Five of the main points are worth mentioning here:

1. To buy or receive any article from a slave, without the consent of his master, in writing, specifying the article, is a highly penal offense.

2. A sale made by a slave, without such written consent, is void, and does not divest the master of his property; he may sue for, and recover it; or he may waive his right to the specific thing, affirm the sale, and recover the price or value, if it was not paid to the slave.

3. A general permission to a slave to go at large and trade for himself as a free man, is contrary to public policy, and a violation of a penal statute. The owner or master of a slave could maintain no action for any claim acquired by a slave while acting under such illegal license.

4. But a slave may be permitted by his master to buy or sell particular articles, and any form of consent or permission given by the master, or his assent after the fact, will give validity to the sale—though the purchaser may be liable to the penalty, if the consent be not in writing.

5. A slave, being authorized by his master to sell any particular thing, becomes the agent of his master for that purpose; and from the authority to sell, an authority to transfer the property, and to fix and receive the price must be inferred; but the slave cannot exercise or receive an authority to maintain any action in relation to it; the right of action for the price belongs to the master, and if he sues, that fact itself is sufficient evidence that he authorized or approved and confirmed the sale.

Unlike the more southerly States, Kentucky did not leave the slave helpless in the courts. If a slave were charged with a capital crime he was brought before the court of quarter sessions, which was composed of the various county

[7] *Littell's Laws*, 2: 116–117.

justices of the peace. They were to constitute a court of oyer and terminer. But they alone were not to decide the fate of the Negro, for the sheriff was required to empanel a jury of twelve men from among the bystanders, who were to constitute the trial jury. It was explicitly stated that legal evidence in such a case would be the confession of the offender, the oath of one or more credible witnesses, or such testimony of Negroes, mulattoes, or Indians as should seem convincing to the court. When a slave was called upon to testify in such a case, the court, the witness "not being a Christian," found it necessary to administer the following charge that he might be under the greater obligation to declare the truth: "You are brought hither as a witness, and by the direction of the law I am to tell you, before you give your evidence, that you must tell the truth and nothing but the truth, and that if it be found hereafter that you tell a lie, and give false testimony in this matter, you must, for so doing, receive thirty-nine lashes on your bare back, well laid on, at the common whipping post."[8]

Section 22 of the law of 1798 provided that the master or owner of any slave might appear in court at a trial of his servant and "make what just defense he can for such slave." The only restriction was that such defense should not interfere with the form of the trial. Naturally the liberally disposed slaveholders interpreted this to mean that they could employ counsel to defend their Negroes and it remained a disputed question down to 1806, when the legislature made the provisions more specific. By this new law it was provided that it was not only the privilege but the duty of the owner of a slave who was being prosecuted to employ an attorney to defend him. The owner neglecting to do so the court must assign counsel to defend the slave and the costs thereby incurred were to be charged to the owner. The fee for defense was not to exceed $200 and if not forthcoming the court was empowered to recover the amount in the manner of any other debt of similar amount.

[8] *Littell's Laws*, 2: 117–118.

It was plainly the intention of the legislature to provide a just trial for any slave, for they even went so far as to enact that the lawyer appointed by the court for the prisoner should "defend such slave as in cases of free persons prosecuted for felony by the laws of this state."[9]

When the slave was convicted of an offense which was punishable by death but which was within the benefit of clergy the capital penalty was not pronounced, but the offender was burnt in the hand or inflicted with any other corporal penalty at the discretion of the court. Should the criminal be sentenced to suffer death, thirty days were to elapse before the execution, except where it was a case of conspiracy, insurrection or rebellion. When the court had decided to sentence the slave to the death penalty a valuation of the Negro was made. This statement was to be turned over to the State auditor of public accounts who was required to issue a warrant on the treasury for the amount in favor of the owner of the convicted party. The owner on his part was to turn over to the treasurer the certificate of the clerk of the court showing that the slave had been condemned and the statement of the sheriff that the offender had been executed or had died before execution.[10]

This matter of the payment to the owner of the value of the executed slave appears never to have been questioned to any extent even by the abolitionists in the legislature until the session of 1830 when a bill was introduced for the repeal of the law. The bill was lost but in the course of the debate it was stated that while Kentucky contained over 160,000 slaves only about one fifth of the tax-paying whites were slaveholders and that $68,000 had already been paid out of the State treasury as indemnity for slaves executed. After the defeat of this bill there was offered a substitute which proposed that a tax of one fourth of one per cent should be levied upon the value of all slaves in the State for the creation of a fund out of which to make such disbursements, but this was likewise lost.[11]

[9] *Littell's Laws*, 3: 403.
[10] *Ibid.*, 2: 117–118.
[11] *Niles' Register*, February 2, 1830.

Until 1811 there were no special enactments on slave crimes and their punishments. The court had, therefore, more or less range in the exactment of penalties but the legislature of 1811 passed during the first fortnight of its session a specific law governing slave crimes. Only four offenses were to be regarded as punishable by death: (1) conspiracy and rebellion, (2) administering poison with intent to kill, (3) voluntary manslaughter and (4) rape of a white woman. If any slaves were to be found guilty of consulting or advising the murder of any one, every such consultation was to constitute an offense and be punishable by any number of stripes not exceeding one hundred.[12]

As time went on the list of capital crimes was increased as a natural result of the growth of the slave population and their growing state of unrest after the incoming of the antislavery propaganda. By the close of the slavery era in Kentucky there were eleven offenses for which slaves should suffer death: (1) murder, (2) arson, (3) rape of a white woman, (4) robbery, (5) burglary, (6) conspiracy, (7) administering poison with intent to kill, (8) manslaughter, (9) attempting to commit rape on a white woman, (10) shooting at a white person with intent to kill, and (11) wounding a white person with intent to kill. It will readily be seen that from a practical standpoint these eleven offenses can be narrowed down to eight. The severity of the slave code can be shown by comparison of the capital crimes for white persons at the same time. These were four in number, (1) murder, (2) carnal abuse of a female under ten years of age, (3) wilful burning of the penitentiary and (4) being an accessory to the fact.[13]

Virginia had early enacted that slaves should be considered as real estate in the settlement of inheritances. But the growing tendency to look upon the slaves in all things else as personal chattels led to such legal and popular confusion that the Virginia assembly often observed that they were "real estate in some respects, personal in others, and

[12] *Littell's Laws*, 4: 223–224.
[13] Stroud, *Laws relating to Slavery*, p. 86.
Littell & Swigert, 2: 1066–9; 1060–4.

both in others." Regardless of such legal complexity it was not until 1793 that it was enacted that "all negro and mulatto slaves in all courts of judicature shall be held and adjudged to be personal estate."

In drawing up the slave code of 1798 Kentucky disregarded the legal experience of Virginia and her more recent remedial legislation and enacted that "all negro, mulatto or Indian slaves, in all courts of judicature and other places within this commonwealth, shall be held, taken and adjudged to be real estate, and shall descend to the heirs and widows of persons departing this life, as lands are directed to descend." It was further provided, however, that "all such slaves shall be liable to the payment of debts, and may be taken by execution for that end, as other chattels, or personal estate may be."[14]

Such a law coupled with the legal precedents of Virginia served to intensify the mixed property conception of the slave. The confusion, however, was purely legal, for slaves were held in all other respects as personalty; but in cases of inheritance and the probation of wills the Kentucky Court of Appeals was often called upon to define clearly the legal status of the Negro in bondage. The first important decision was handed down in 1824 in the case of Chinn and wife *vs.* Respass, in which it was pointed out that while slaves were by law made real estate for the purpose of descent and dower, yet they had in law many of the attributes of personal estate. They would pass by a nuncupative will, and lands would not; they could be limited in a grant or devise no otherwise than personal chattels; and personal actions might be brought to recover the possession of them.

[14] It would perhaps be well to point out here the general common-law difference between the treatment of real and personal estate in a will. The title of the personal property of the deceased is vested in the executor and he holds it for the payment of debts and distribution according to the will of the testator. On the other hand the real estate vests in the devisees or heirs and does not go to the administrator, unless by statute enactment, which was in part true in Kentucky, in the case above, where the slaves, although real estate, were held liable for the debts of their master. *Littell's Laws,* 2: 120.

Furthermore "they were in their nature personal estate, being moveable property, and as such might attend the person of the proprietor wherever he went; and in practice they were so considered by the people in general."[15]

Conversely, the court was often called upon to interpret the phrase "personal estate" in wills and contracts, where it appeared without any other restrictive expression or provision, and it consistently held that the term should be construed as embracing slaves.[16] Gradually the personal property conception began to secure even legal precedence over that of real estate when the two interpretations came into close conflict. This was accomplished by placing more stress on the proviso in the original slave code, which placed slaves in the hands of the administrator as assets for the payment of debts. This led to increasing power for the executor who could even defeat the title of the heirs, though the property may have been specifically devised. Hence it was not surprising that in the Revised Statutes of 1852 it was provided that slaves should thereafter be deemed and held as personal estate. Coming after all doubt of the personalty of slaves had been removed by the decisions of the highest tribunal in the State, this law meant little more than the repeal of the old statute making slaves real estate.

The wonder is that Kentucky should have chosen to hold to an antiquated legal conception for fifty years after Virginia had proved its fallacy by her experience in the eighteenth century. While it did little harm, it had few advantages. The existence of the theory was chiefly noticeable in the frequent legal battles over technicalities in the settlement of estates. In the popular mind slaves were always considered personal property, and the spirit of the slave code itself embodied that conception as regarded all things save the question of inheritance.

With respect to the liberty of the slaves the code of

[15] *T. B. Monroe's Report I.*, 23.
[16] Beatty *vs.* Judy, 1 Dana, 101.
Plumpton *vs.* Cook, 2 A. K. Marshall, 450.

1798 clearly shows that the existing type of slavery was purely rural, for the restrictions on slaves concerned only the plantation Negroes. Strictly understood, the slave was not to leave the farm of his owner without a pass from his master, the main purpose being to keep the Negroes from congregating on any one farm. Later when emissaries from the North became unusually active the rights and privileges of the slaves were further restricted. This change was due to the current belief that these foreign individuals were bent upon stirring up strife among the slaves and inciting them to insurrection. Once started such a scheme would have resulted in anarchy especially in the towns. The real curbing provisions were not started until along in the thirties when these outside forces had begun to make their appearance in the urban communities.[17]

In some parts of the State were instituted mounted patrols, who went about at night and watched the movement of slaves. They were to apprehend any servant who was caught away from his home plantation without a pass from his master.[18] Such an institution was based on good Negro psychology, for his fear of the spirits of night was well known. Citizens of that time have told us many tales of the dread which the slave had of meeting these night raiders whom they termed "patter-rollers" and how they came to sing of them in true Negro fashion:

> Over the fence and through the paster,
> Run, nigger, run, oh, run a little faster,
> Run, nigger, run,
> The patter-roller ketch you.

Such a system of county patrols did not prove to be sufficient as the slave population grew and the towns became larger and more attractive to the country slave. The legislature of 1834 in drawing up a law concerning tavern keepers had this problem clearly in mind when they provided that no person should sell, give or loan any spirituous liquors to

[17] Rothert, *History of Muhlenburg County*, p. 343.
[18] Young, B. H., *History of Jessamine County*, p. 89.

slaves, other than his own, under a penalty of $10 for each offense. Furthermore, if the offender was a licensed liquor dealer, he should have his license taken away from him for the term of two years.[19] That even this measure did not prove effective enough to curb the evil of Negroes congregating in the towns is shown by the further provision passed March 6, 1850, to increase the fine to $50 for each offense.[20] A still further extension was that of February 27, 1856, which provided that free Negroes were to be included in the restriction unless they presented a certificate from "some white person of respectable character." No slaves or free Negroes were to be employed in the selling or distribution of liquor nor were they to be allowed to visit or even loaf around any place where intoxicants were kept for sale.[21] The session of 1858 made the force of the law more explicit by defining very clearly the jurisdiction in such cases.[22]

Not only the State authorities but the towns as well were active in the measures adopted to meet the growing problem. The best available sample of the many provisions which the town councils drew up is this one which was passed by the trustees of Henderson in 1840:

> It shall be and is hereby made, the duty of the Town Sergeant or either of his assistants, to punish with any number of lashes not exceeding ten, all or any negro slave or slaves who may be found in any grog shop, grocery or other place where spirituous liquors are retailed in said town, or who may be found on the streets of said town after ten o'clock at night, unless it shall appear to the said Town Sergeant, or assistant, that said negro slave or slaves, are acting under the orders of his, her or their master or mistress, and it shall further be the duty of the Town Sergeant, or either of his assistants, to enter into any grog shop, grocery or other place where spirituous liquors are retailed, in said town, whenever he shall be informed that any negro slave or slaves are collected therein. Provided, said Town Sergeant, or assistant, can enter the same peaceably and without force.[23]

[19] Session Laws, 1834, p. 726.
[20] *Ibid.*, 1850, p. 51.
[21] *Ibid.*, 1856, Vol. 1, pp. 42–44.
[22] *Ibid.*, 1858, Vol. 1, pp. 47–48.
[23] Starling, p. 290.

This town regulation offers perhaps another proof of the oft-repeated statement regarding the slave laws of Kentucky that while they appeared severe on the statute books they were always mild in the enforcement. The regulation of the movement of slaves in the towns was always subject to the local conditions. Beginning about 1850 there was a growing feeling in some of the more thickly populated sections of the State that the type of Negro slave who sought to frequent the village saloons would sooner or later start an insurrection. But no such uprising ever occurred and the fear of such seems to have been due to the current animosity towards the activities of the abolitionists, which was prevalent throughout the State.

In the course of time it was considered necessary to treat more seriously also the importation of slaves. The advisability of preventing the importation of bondmen had been foreseen in Kentucky from the experience of the mother State of Virginia which had enacted a stringent law in 1778 imposing a penalty of one thousand pounds and the forfeiture of the slave upon the importer of any into that commonwealth. The ninth article of the Kentucky Constitution of 1792 had provided that the legislature "shall have full power to prevent slaves being brought into this commonwealth as merchandise; they shall have full power to prevent any slave being brought into this state from a foreign country, and to prevent those from being brought into this state, who have been since the first of January, 1789, or may hereafter be imported into any of the United States from a foreign country."[24]

The session of the State assembly in 1794 drew up a law concerning the importation and emancipation of slaves but it was largely a mere modification of the law of the State of Virginia. It was not until the adoption of the slave code of 1798 that the question was firmly settled by a more definite statement. By article 25 of that act it was provided "that no slave or slaves shall be imported into this state

[24] *Littell's Laws*, 1: 32.

from any foreign country, nor shall any slave who has been imported into the United States from any foreign country since the first day of January, 1789, or may hereafter be imported into the United States from any foreign country under the penalty of $300."

This was merely carrying out the provisions of the constitution. Section 26 provided that "no slave or slaves shall be imported into this state as merchandise, and any person offending herein, shall frofeit and pay the sum of $300 for each slave so imported, to be recovered by action of debt or information, in any court having cognizance of the same, one half to the prosecutor, the other half to the use of the commonwealth." More significant was the proviso that "this act shall not extend to prevent any citizen of this state bringing for his own use, provided, they have not been brought into the United States from any foreign country since January 1, 1789; nor shall it be construed to prevent persons emigrating to this state bringing their slaves with them, but either a citizen of this state or persons emigrating to this state may bring slaves not prohibited by this act."[25]

An act of 1814 amended the above by prohibiting the importation of slaves by any of the emigrants if they did not intend to settle in Kentucky.[26] An attempt was made by a law of February 8, 1815, to remedy some of the defects which had been found. The legal penalty for importation was increased to $600 for each slave imported and a fine of $200 was added for every person buying or selling such slave. No indictment was to be subject to a shorter limitation than five years and once so accused no person was to be discharged or acquitted unless he could produce evidence to show that within sixty days of his arrival in Kentucky he had deposited the following oath, duly signed, in the county clerk's office where he resides: "I, ..., do swear that my removal to the state of Kentucky was with the intention of becoming

[25] *Littell's Laws*, 2: 119.
[26] *Ibid.*, 5: 293.

The Legal Status of Slavery

a citizen thereof, and that I have brought no slave or slaves to this state, with the intention of selling them."[27]

It is evident from all contemporary discussions of the question of importation that it was the firm conviction that in order to do justice to the slave and the institution as a whole within the State it was necessary to prevent the infusion of any foreign slave element. Once such a policy had been carried out to a successful conclusion, they would have been confronted only with a purely domestic type of slavery and its increase. With such an ideal condition, for those times, the institution eventually would have been easily handled. But these early lawmakers, while no doubt honest in their intentions, did not have the wisdom that was tempered with experience, and the unscrupulous slave traders found further defects in the law and took advantage of them. A careful examination of the law of 1794, the codification of 1798, and the amendments of 1814 and 1815 will show that the whole theory of non-importation is summed up in the word *intent*. It was the intent with which the slaves were introduced, and to this alone the penalty attached. They were not to be imported as merchandise but every citizen could import slaves for his own use. Once these slaves were within the State there was no penalty provided if they were sold. There was nothing to prevent a man from selling what slaves he had imported and later going without the confines of the State and bringing in more. If he were brought before the court, he would claim that he had not intended to sell them when they were brought in, and no one could place a penalty on his intentions. It seems that there were other violators of the spirit of the law, who never sold any of the slaves but brought them into the State in large numbers and then hired them out for such long terms as 99 years.[28] The fundamental idea of the law had been to place a curb on the increase of the slave population by importation and these acts were in direct opposition to the intention of the enactments.

[27] *Ibid.*, 5: 435–437.
[28] Barre, W. L., *Speeches and Writings of Thomas F. Marshall*, p. 115.

An index of the inefficiency of the existing provisions regarding importation can be found in the figures on the growth of the slave population during this period when it is borne in mind that legally slaves could not be imported, except for personal use, after the year 1794. The slave population in 1790 had been 11,830 and by 1800 had increased to 40,343 or at the rate of 241.02 per cent; in 1810 there were 80,561 slaves or an increase of 99.69 per cent; in 1820 there were 126,732, a gain of 57.31 per cent; and by 1830 they had increased 30.36 per cent to a total of 165,213. During the same period there was a great increase in the white population but it was always from 20 per cent to 40 per cent below that of the slaves. It appears that the law prohibiting importation was not as effective as it should have been. While none of the statesmen appear to have figured from the statistical viewpoint there was no end of discussion regarding the necessity of extending the law to include more than the question of intent at the time of importation.

The avowed resolution of Kentucky to deal with the slavery question in the most humane manner and to stop any unscrupulous dealing in slaves for the mere sake of profit is nowhere more clearly shown than in the firm action which was taken not only in the court room but in the legislative halls when it was found that advantage had been taken of the letter of the law at the expense of its spirit. On February 2, 1833, the legislature passed a law prohibiting all importation of slaves even for personal use. The only exception provided in this case was that emigrants were allowed to bring in slaves, if they took the oath that had been provided in the law of 1815. The evil mentioned above brought about by hiring slaves for excessively long terms was prohibited by declaring illegal any contract which extended beyond one year and exacting a penalty of $600 for each offense. This law of 1833 was destined to be the crux of many a heated argument for the remainder of the slavery period. Many a candidate for office during the next thirty years rose to victory or fell in defeat because of his position with regard to this one statute of the State. It was the briefest of all the enactments on the slavery question but it was by far the most important and far-reaching provision that the legislature ever enacted in connection with the institution.[29]

It is noticeable that this measure was not brought about in any sense by the activities of the abolitionists, for they had not at that time made their appearance in the State. It was an honest endeavor on the part of the native population, slaveholding as well as non-slaveholding, to carry out the spirit of their State constitution which had been adopted back in 1792. Thomas F. Marshall, who later was the leader of the Lexington group which removed Cassius M. Clay's *True American* to Cincinnati, has borne testimony to the fact that the slaveholding element voted for the law of 1833. "At the time of the passage of this law," said he, "the sect known by the title of 'abolitionists' had not made their appearance. And, as I was sworn then upon the constitution of my country, by all the obligations of that oath, I affirm now that I do not believe that the principles and designs ascribed to that party were in the contemplation of any human being who voted for the law. I was myself not only never an abolitionist, but never an emancipationist upon any plan which I ever heard proposed."[30]

But the question was not settled for all time, for with the coming of the abolitionist element there was a general tendency throughout the State to enact stricter laws governing slaves. Many who had voted for the enactment began to cry for a repeal of the law, but it was not until the session of 1841 that it was seriously debated in the general assembly.

[29] Section 1 of the law 1833 read: "Each and every person or persons who shall hereafter import into this state any slave or slaves, or who shall sell or buy, or contract for the sale or purchase, for a longer term than one year, of the service of any such slave or slaves, knowing the same to have been imported, shall forfeit and pay $600 for each slave so imported, sold, or bought, or whose service has been so contracted for; recoverable by indictment of a grand jury or any action of debt, in the name of the Commonwealth in any circuit court, where the offenders may be found." Session Laws, 1833, pp. 258–261.

[30] Barre, W. L., p. 116.

Then after a long and ardent discussion in the House of Representatives a vote was taken on the ninth of January—with 34 in favor of the repeal and 53 against it. Never within the previous decade had a bill before the House produced such popular interest.[31] It came up in the Senate at the session of 1843 but after another warm debate it failed by a vote of 14 to 21. Sentiment for the repeal continued to grow and in 1849 the law was amended so as "no longer to prohibit persons from purchasing and bringing into the State slaves for their own use."[32] This changed the situation back to what it was before 1833, for it will be recalled that the main feature of the law of 1833 compared with that of 1815 was the prohibition of importation even for personal use. It could easily have been predicted that such an amendment would pass, for the legislature of 1847 had passed 27 distinct resolutions granting to as many individuals the right to import slaves for personal use. The session of 1848 made 24 similar provisions.

This apparently radical swing towards the side of the slave owner in 1849 was more than likely brought about by the very intense campaign which was carried on by the emancipationists. Such a movement served to unite the slave forces against any attack upon the institution. This tendency was shown not only in the halls of the State legislature but in the constitutional convention which met later in the same year. Although the abolitionists had looked forward to some advanced constitutional provisions on emancipation and the inclusion of the law of 1833 in the organic law of the State they were astounded to be met with the virtual repeal of that statute by the legislature. On the other hand the constitutional convention not only rejected bodily all the reform measures but added to the Bill of Rights this extraordinary amendment: "The right of property is before and higher than any constitutional sanction, and the right of the owner of a slave to such slave and its increase is the same and as inviolable as the right of the owner of any property whatsoever."

[31] *Niles' Register*, January 23, 1841.
[32] Collins, Vol. 1, p. 83.

The slave trader once more had the courage to appear in the State. Richard Henry Collins in an editorial in the *Maysville Eagle,* November 6, 1849, gives us some vivid evidence of the effect which the repeal of the law of 1833 had had in a few weeks' time. "A remarkably forcible and practical argument in favor of incorporating the negro law of 1833 into the new constitution reached this city in bodily shape on Sunday, per the steamer *Herman* from Charleston, Virginia. Forty-four negroes—men, women and children —of whom seventeen men had handcuffs on one hand and were chained together, two and two, passed through this city for the interior of the State, under charge of two regular traders. We opine that few who saw the spectacle would hereafter say aught against the readoption of the anti-importation act of 1833." Such scenes as this were the result of the passage of an innocent-looking measure which allowed citizens to import slaves for their own use, but which could really be made to include almost any influx of slaves.

No further change in the importation laws was made until the crisis immediately preceding the Civil War, when practically all opposition was removed and the law of 1833 was abolished in its entirety.[33] Explanations of the sudden turn of mind are not hard to find for the enactment was passed amid the turmoil and chaos brought on by an impending war and the radical slaveholders found it easy to get votes for their side in a last vain endeavor to save the institution, not so much from an economic standpoint as from a matter of principle. The last chapter in the legal history of the importation problem in Kentucky, however, had not yet been written. After three years of the armed conflict between the North and the South, Kentucky, which had remained loyal to the Union and fought against the slave power of the South, reenacted on February 2, 1864, the old law of 1798 on the prohibition of the importation of slaves.[34] The wording was somewhat different, but the

[33] Session Laws, 1860, Vol. 1, p. 104.
[34] *Ibid.*, 1864, pp. 70–72.

essential provisions were the same. Coming at such a time, it never had any significance in the slavery problem in the State, but it is interesting as one of the last vain efforts of the institution before it was mustered out of the State by an amendment to the federal constitution, which was passed without the assent of the State legislature of Kentucky.

No less serious than the question of importation was the problem of the fugitive slave. This has been treated many times and every discussion of it has involved much of what transpired in Kentucky or on its borders. It is not the purpose here to repeat any of that story because it belongs rather to the anti-slavery field, and, furthermore, has been recently very well treated by A. E. Martin in his *Antislavery Movement in Kentucky*. We are here concerned with the legal phase of the fugitive problem as it existed in Kentucky throughout this period, as an internal question; in the relation between the State and other States; and between the State and the federal authorities. In so far as it relates to the law within the State such a discussion naturally divides itself into two phases—those measures which affected the fugitive slave himself, and those which were directed towards conspirators who might have brought about the escape of slaves. The former group of laws were enacted, for the most part, in the early days of statehood, for a runaway slave was a natural evil in any condition of servitude. The latter group of measures were passed in the later days of the institution when the anti-slavery propagandists came in from the North, for until then there were no cases of enticement. A large majority of those who were placed on trial for conspiracy in the history of slavery in Kentucky proved to be outsiders who had come into the State after 1835. The citizens of the commonwealth who were opposed to the institution were satisfied to confine themselves to mere words advocating the emancipation of slaves.

The State early adopted the slave code of Virginia in regard to the treatment of runaway slaves just as it did in regard to the general legal rights of the bonded Negro but provided more drastic regulations in 1798. Any person who suspected a Negro of being a runaway slave could take him before a justice of the peace, and swear to his belief in the guilt of the accused. Being provided with a certificate from the justice where he found the slave, the apprehender could then take the fugitive back to the owner and might collect ten shillings as a reward and an additional shilling for each mile of travel necessary in bringing the slave to the master. If the money should not be paid, the person entitled to it could recover the sum in any court of record in the State upon the production of his certificate of apprehension as legal evidence.[35]

In many cases the runaway could not be identified as the property of any particular owner, so provision was made for the commitment of the offender to the county jail. The keeper was forthwith to post a bulletin on the courthouse with a complete description of the Negro. If at the end of two months no claimant appeared the sheriff was to publish an advertisement in the *Lexington Gazette* for three consecutive months so that the news of capture would reach a larger public. In the meantime the sheriff was authorized to hire out the fugitive and the wages thus received were to pay for the reward of the captor and the expenses incurred by the county officials. If the owner appeared during the period and proved his property, he could have the slave at once in spite of any labor contract, providing he would pay any excess of expenses over wages received. But often the master never appeared and if a year had expired since the last advertisement had been published in the *Gazette*, the sheriff could sell the slave and place the proceeds of the sale plus the wages received over the expenses, in the county treasury. This sum was credited to the unknown owner, for if he should appear at any future time the county would reimburse him for his loss, otherwise the fund reverted to the county.[36]

[35] *Littell's Laws*, 2: 5–6.
[36] *Ibid.*, 2: 5–6.

This legal code for the apprehension of runaway slaves remained practically unchanged throughout the period of slavery. The only amendments which were ever made were those for the increase of the reward to the captor and it is significant that the first of these changes did not come until more than a generation later in 1835. Then the compensation was divided into three classes: for those captured in their own county, $10; in another county, $20; out of the State, $30.[37] Just three years later it was found necessary to increase this by the following interesting law: "The compensation for apprehending fugitive slaves taken without this commonwealth, and in a State where slavery is not tolerated by law, shall be one hundred dollars, on the delivery to the owner at his residence within this commonwealth, and seventy-five dollars if lodged in the jail of any county in this commonwealth, and the owner be notified so as to be able to reclaim the slave."[38] There were no more advances until a law of March 3, 1860, increased the reward to one hundred and fifty dollars if the slave were caught outside the State and brought back to the home county; one hundred and twenty-five dollars if caught outside the State and brought back to any county in Kentucky; and twenty dollars if caught anywhere in the home county.

The trend of these laws, from the viewpoint of the rewards alone, shows the increasing importance of the fugitive problem to the slaveholding group. It is noticeable that from the year 1798 until 1835 there was not sufficient pressure upon the State legislature to increase the reward to the captor of a runaway. It is further evident from the scarcity of contemporary advertisements that there were comparatively few Negroes who ventured forth from the neighborhood of their masters. But with the rise of the anti-slavery movement in the North and the growth of abolition sentiment as expressed by the apostles of Negro freedom who had come from across the Ohio, the slaves tended to run away in ever-increasing numbers. This was soon

[37] Session Laws, 1835, pp. 82–83.
[38] *Ibid.*, 1838, p. 158.

followed by a more rigid policy of apprehension upon the part of the Kentucky legal authorities, apparent in the increasing reward.

Not all cases of fugitives were to be reached by a mere system of capture and reward. Rarely did a slave make his escape into a free State without the aid of some one in sympathy with him. Hence the need for legal machinery to punish those who assisted runaways. From a chronological point of view the laws governing such cases divide themselves into two parts; in the early days they refer to those who would help a slave who had already escaped; in the later period they were directed towards those who induced slaves to leave their home plantations.

Whichever of the free States he tried to reach it was necessary for the Negro to cross the Ohio River to get to his haven of refuge. If the Kentucky authorities could prevent him from crossing the stream on the northern and western boundary, they could prevent any slave from making a successful escape. Consequently the legislature as early as 1823 attempted to solve the problem by passing a law forbidding masters of vessels and others from employing and removing Negroes out of the State.[39] This act prevented runaways from securing work on a steamboat with the specific purpose of leaving once they were on free soil. But as usual this enactment was not effective, because there was a loop-hole in it. The State assembly in 1831, therefore, provided that no ferryman on the Ohio River should transport slaves across from Kentucky. No other person, not owning or keeping a ferry, was to be permitted to set slaves over, or to loan them boats or watercraft. Slaves could only cross the river when they had the written consent of their masters. Each and every owner of a ferry was required to give bond in the sum of $3,000 to carry out the spirit of the law; and for every violation he was subject to a fine of $200.[40]

[39] Session Laws, 1823, p. 178.
[40] Ibid., 1831–2, pp. 54–55.

Not content with their previous efforts the general assembly of 1838 went still further and prohibited slaves from going as passengers on mail stages or coaches anywhere within the State, except upon the written request of their owners, or in the master's company. The liability for the enforcement of the law rested upon the stage proprietors, who were to be fined $100 for each slave illegally transported.[41]

No stringent laws were made against the enticement of slaves to run away until 1830 when the abolitionists first began to appear. Until that time there seems to have been no need for any legal enactment regarding the question. The only trouble previously had been with the whites and free Negroes who aided a slave already on his way to the North. It was in response to the popular demand that on Jaunary 28, 1830, the State legislature provided severe penalties for any person found guilty of (1) enticing a slave to leave his owner, (2) furnishing a forged paper of freedom, (3) assisting a slave to escape out of the State, (4) enticing a slave to run away, or (5) concealing a runaway slave. Should a person be suspected of any one of these offenses and not be found guilty, he was to give security for his good behavior to avoid all accusation in the future.[42]

The most interesting legal case based on this law was that of Delia Webster, a young lady from Vermont, who was tried in the Fayette Circuit Court in December, 1844, for the enticement of a Negro slave boy from Lexington. The details of the trial show that the court was just and fair in spite of the fact that both Miss Webster and her copartner, Calvin Fairbank, were not citizens of the State and had furthermore used all kinds of deceit to accomplish their purpose. For the sake of aiding one Negro slave boy to reach freedom they went to the expense and trouble to feign an elopement to Ohio via Maysville, but the Lexington authorities caught them as they were coming back on the Lexington Pike near Paris. At the trial it was shown

[41] Session Laws, 1838, p. 155.
[42] *Ibid.*, 1830, pp. 173–175.

The Legal Status of Slavery

that Fairbank was in Kentucky for no other reason than to induce slaves to escape to the North and that Miss Webster had come to Lexington as a school teacher merely as a cloak for her abolitionist work. The evidence offered by the prosecution was damaging in the extreme. The defense put forth no data for her side at all, evidently preferring to be hailed as a martyr to the cause for which she stood. The jury brought in a verdict of guilty and she was sentenced to serve two years in the State penitentiary.[43]

The young accomplice, Calvin Fairbank, proved to be the most persistent abolitionist the Kentucky authorities ever encountered. He pleaded guilty to the indictment as charged and was sentenced to serve 15 years in the penitentiary, to which he was taken February 18, 1845. Evidently convinced that he had been punished sufficiently Governor John J. Crittenden pardoned him August 23, 1849, on condition that he leave the State at once.[44] But such an ardent young enthusiast for the cause of Negro freedom soon found that there were other slaves who were in need of his aid and on November 3, 1851, he came across from Jeffersonville to Louisville under the cover of night and "kidnapped" a young mulatto woman who had been doomed to be sold at auction.[45] Presumably in the hope of rescuing other slaves he remained in the vicinity for several days until on the morning of November 9 he was arrested by the Kentucky authorities. Fairbank was placed in jail pending his trial, which took place in the following March, when he was again sentenced to serve 15 years at hard labor in the State penitentiary. He began his term March 9, 1852.[46] This time he was not so fortunate in an early release. The chief executives of the State from time to time refused to pardon him. In April, 1864, Governor Bramlette was called to Washington by President Lincoln for a

[43] *Western Law Journal*, 2: 232–235 (best report of the trial).
Niles' Register, December 21, 1844.
Webster, Delia A., *Kentucky Jurisprudence*, pp. 1–84.
[44] Fairbank, *How the Way was Prepared*, pp. 53, 57.
[45] *Ibid.*, p. 85.
[46] *Ibid.*, p. 103.

conference and Richard T. Jacobs, the Lieutenant-Governor, became the acting Governor. This son-in-law of Thomas H. Benton had taken more or less pity on Fairbank, for he had stated to the prisoner that if he ever became the chief executive he would release him. The opportunity thus being presented for the first time, Jacob pardoned Fairbank on April 15, 1864, after a continuous imprisonment of twelve years. Such was the experience in Kentucky of an ardent northern abolitionist who boasted that he had "liberated forty-seven slaves from hell."[47]

The systematic stealing of slaves from Kentucky had begun about 1841 and at the time of the Webster and Fairbank trial was at its height. This movement was one of the results growing out of the animosity created by another legal case which occurred in 1838—that of the Rev. John B. Mahan of Brown County, Ohio. This Methodist minister, although living in the State of Ohio, was indicted by the grand jury of Mason County, Kentucky, for having aided in the escape of certain slaves. Governor Clark, of Kentucky, then issued a requisition on the Governor of Ohio for Mahan as a "fugitive from justice." Upon receipt of the demand, the chief executive of Ohio immediately issued a warrant for the arrest of the minister. A short time later he became convinced that this step had been too hasty, because Mahan had never been in Kentucky. His offense had merely consisted in helping runaways along the "underground railroad," once they were on free soil.

Hence, Governor Vance sent a special messenger to the chief executive of Kentucky redemanding the alleged fugitive from justice. Governor Clark made this very cordial and diplomatic reply:

> The position assumed by you in relation to the fact of Mahan having never been within the limits of Kentucky is clearly correct, and if upon the legal investigation of the case it be found true, he will doubtless be acquitted. I feel great solicitude that this citizen of your state, who has been arrested and brought to Kentucky,

[47] Fairbank, pp. 144, 149.

upon my requisition, shall receive ample and full justice, and that, if upon legal investigation he be found innocent of the crime alleged against him, he shall be released and set at liberty. I will, therefore, address a letter to the judge and commonwealth attorney of the Mason Circuit, communicating to them the substance of your letter, and the evidence which you have transmitted to me.[48]

The efforts of the Governor of Ohio were eventually successful, for in spite of his slaveholding sympathies Governor Clark wrote to the judge of the Mason Circuit and the latter charged the jury in no uncertain terms regarding the jurisdiction in the case. After a trial of six days Mahan was acquitted.

The importance of this case does not rest in the trial and its events but rather in the reactions which it had upon the Kentucky populace. No one doubted that Mahan was guilty of aiding slaves; but it was seen that he had been shrewd enough to confine his activities to the State of Ohio, where the Kentucky authorities had no jurisdiction. In his opening message to the State legislature, which met the next month after the acquittal of Mahan, Governor Clark voiced the sentiment of a large majority of Kentuckians. Bear in mind that these words came from the same man who a month before had advised the Circuit judge of the illegality of the Mahan indictment.

Some of the abolitionists of an adjoining state, not contented with the mere promulgation of opinions and views calculated to excite a feeling of disaffection among our slave population, and to render this description of property insecure in the hands of its proprietors, have extended their operations so far as to mingle personally with our slaves, to enter into arrangements with them, and to afford them the means and facilities to escape from their owners. This flagitious conduct is not to be tolerated—it must be checked in its origin by the adoption of efficient and energetic measures, or it will, in all human probability, lead to results greatly to be deprecated by every friend to law and order. This demon-like spirit that rages uncontrolled by law, or sense of moral right, must be

[48] *American Anti-slavery Society Report*, 1839, p. 90.

overcome—it must be subdued; its action in the state should be prohibited under such penalties as will effectually curb its lawlessness and disarm its power.[49]

In pursuance of this and similar recommendations the State legislature early in 1839 despatched a delegation of members to the general assembly of Ohio then meeting at Columbus. These men were charged to secure a law in Ohio for the better security of Kentucky fugitive slave property. The Kentucky officials had always been confronted with the problem of recovering runaways captured in Ohio, even when they personally knew the captive. The old law of 1807 in Ohio was never lax in the enforcement, but the plea of habeas corpus was habitually used for the defendant and, furthermore, it often happened that the necessary proofs of ownership were not in evidence. These facts coupled with the publicity of the Mahan trial brought about the peculiar legislative commission from Kentucky.

Here was a delegation from a slave commonwealth sent to a free State to demand a rigorous fugitive slave law for their own benefit. The Kentucky committee went even further and suggested the provisions of the proposed enactment—and the remarkable thing was that they actually succeeded. Although Ohio was known to be the home of anti-slavery interests the law passed without any difficulty. By its provisions a slave owner or his agent could appear before any judge, justice or mayor, who was authorized to issue a warrant to any sheriff in Ohio calling upon him to arrest the fugitive and bring him before any judge in the county where caught. Upon proof of his ownership to the court the owner was entitled to a certificate for removal. A heavy fine and imprisonment were the penalty for any interference with the execution of either the warrant or the removal of the slave. The vote on this measure in the House of Representatives was 53 to 15. There has been made an analysis of this roll call, which shows that the opposition all came from northern Ohio—whereas those in

[49] *American Anti-slavery Society Report*, 1839, pp. 93–94.

the southern part of the State voted for it because they were not inclined to allow any disturbance of the friendly commercial relationship which they had with their neighbor State to the south. Moreover, they objected to their locality being used as a place of refuge for unfortunate Negroes.[50]

Henceforth Ohio became a veritable hunting ground for fugitive slaves, but the wiser of the Negroes and the abolitionists diverted their efforts to other fields of escape, especially through Indiana and Illinois. The legal authorities at this time began to realize that their hope lay in the enactment of a federal law but no definite steps were taken until after the affair of Francis Troutman at Marshall, Michigan, in January, 1847. Troutman came from Kentucky to Michigan to bring back six runaways that had been located at Marshall. When he had found them and was about to take them before a magistrate for identification, a crowd of citizens of the town put in their appearance and threatened injury to Troutman and his three Kentucky companions. Although the latter were acting in accordance with the law the mob would not let them proceed in any manner—not even to appear before the magistrate—but demanded that they leave town within two hours. In the meantime they were all four arrested, tried and found guilty of trespass.[51] When these events were reported back to Kentucky mass meetings were held throughout the State in protest against the Michigan action. The State legislature drew up a resolution calling upon Congress to enact a new fugitive slave law.[52] The Senate referred the petition to the Committee on Judiciary and they later reported a new fugitive slave bill which was read twice and then pigeonholed. The same action was repeated at the next session in 1849.

The general feeling in Kentucky was intensified just at this time by a decision of the United States Supreme Court in the case of Jones *vs.* Van Zandt, which had been pending in various courts for five years. In April, 1842, John Van

[50] Chaddock, F. E., *Ohio before 1850*, p. 86.
[51] McMaster, *History of the United States*, Vol. 7: 262–263.
[52] Senate Document No. 19, 30th Congress, 1st Session.

Zandt, a former Kentuckian, then living in Springdale just north of Cincinnati, was caught in the act of aiding nine fugitive slaves to escape, and one of them got away even from the slave catchers. Consequently Wharton Jones, the Kentucky owner, brought suit against Van Zandt in the U. S. Circuit Court under the federal fugitive slave act of 1793 for $500 for concealing and harboring a fugitive slave. The jury returned a verdict for the plaintiff in the sum of $1,200 as damages on two other counts in addition to the penalty of $500 for concealing and harboring. Salmon P. Chase was the lawyer for Van Zandt and in a violent attack on the law 1793 he appealed to the U. S. Supreme Court on the grounds that this statute was repugnant to the Constitution of the United States and to the sixth article of the Ordinance of 1787. Van Zandt in the appeal had the advantage of the services of William H. Seward in addition to Chase while Jones was represented by Senator Morehead, of Kentucky. Justice Levi Woodbury in rendering the decision of the court sustained all the judgments against Van Zandt and denied that the law of 1793 was opposed to either the Constitution or the Ordinance of 1787.[53]

At last the people of Kentucky had secured a firm ruling from the highest judicial authority on the force of the existing laws. Cold reason in the light of that day, apart from all anti-slavery propaganda, justified them in making these demands. Henceforth, there was no doubt about the legality of their position—it was a question merely of the illegal opposition to the return of fugitives from the States to the North. The Troutman case and many others, however, had served as an index of northern sentiment in the matter, for the troubles of the Kentucky slaveholder were just beginning. A year later, in 1848, a requisition was issued on the Governor of Ohio for the return of fifteen persons charged with aiding in the escape of slaves. Imagine the feeling in Kentucky when Governor Bell of Ohio positively refused to give these persons up, stating that the laws of

[53] 5 Howard's Reports, 215–232.

Ohio did not recognize man as property. It was apparently a political move on his part, for there was no question of the property conception of slavery involved whatsoever. He acted in direct opposition to the laws of his State enacted in 1839 and to the federal fugitive slave law of 1793.

After two decades of struggle the abolitionists had come into their own and it was almost impossible to recover slaves who had run away in spite of the legal machinery that had been set up. Furthermore, the more extreme abolitionists had disregarded all law, orders and rights of private property and had even gone so far as to proclaim that there was a "higher law than the Constitution." Against such a powerful foe the forces of all parties in Kentucky united in a firm stand, demanding more stringent measures. The Supreme Court had decided that the existing law was sufficient to recover fugitives and to demand and secure damages for the interference with that right. With the coming of new conditions, however, it was realized on all sides that new and most extreme measures were necessary.

The existing circumstances are well shown by the attitude of Henry Clay, senator from Kentucky as well as author of the Compromise of 1850. Noted for his leanings towards the North, throughout his public career of more than half a century, and as far back as 1798 the advocate of gradual emancipation in Kentucky, he felt called upon in this crisis to express the irritation of his own people:

I have very little doubt, indeed, that the extent of loss to the state of Kentucky, in consequence of the escape of her slaves is greater, at least in proportion to the total number of slaves that are held within that commonwealth, even than in Virginia. I know full well, and so does the honorable senator from Ohio know, that it is at the utmost hazard and insecurity to life itself, that a Kentuckian can cross the river and go into the interior to take back his fugitive slave from whence he fled. Recently an example occurred even in the city of Cincinnati in respect to one of our most respectable citizens. Not having visited Ohio at all, but Covington, on the opposite side of the river, a little slave of his escaped over to Cincinnati. He pursued it; he found it in the house in which it was concealed; he took it out, and it was rescued by the violence and force of a negro mob from his possession—the police of the city standing by, and either unwilling or unable to afford the assistance which was requisite to enable him to recover his property.

Upon this subject I do think that we have just and serious cause of complaint against the free states. I think they fail in fulfilling a great obligation, and the failure is precisely upon one of those subjects which in its nature is the most irritating and inflaming to those who live in the slave states.[54]

The Fugitive Slave Law of 1793 was superseded by that of 1850 by a sort of political bargaining on the other measures of the Compromise. The letter of the new law was not much different from the one of 1793—the chief changes being in the exaction of severer penalties and the transfer of jurisdiction to the federal courts. But even if members from the North did vote for the new provision there was no public sentiment in the North back of its enforcement. Everyone in Kentucky was heartily in favor of it, but that mattered little. The effectiveness of any fugitive slave law depended upon the spirit in which it was met in the North, for it was there that the law was to be applied. It remained for a more or less forgotten decision of the Supreme Court in 1861 to show the greatest weakness of all laws for the recovery of runaway slaves in the North.

In October, 1859, the Woodford County (Kentucky) grand jury returned an indictment against Willis Lago, a free Negro, charging him with the seduction and enticement of Charlotte, a Negro slave, from her owner, C. W. Nickols. A copy of this indictment certified and authenticated according to the federal law was presented to the Governor of Ohio by the authorized agent of the Governor of Kentucky and the arrest and delivery of the fugitive from justice demanded. The Governor of Ohio referred the matter to the Attorney-General of the State and upon his

[54] Colton, Reed and McKinley, *Works of Henry Clay*, Vol. 3: 329.

advice the chief executive refused to deliver up the Negro. The Supreme Court having original jurisdiction in suits between two States, the demand for a mandamus to compel the Governor of Ohio to deliver Lago to the Kentucky authorities was heard by that body in a suit under the title of Kentucky *vs.* Dennison (the Governor of Ohio). The decision of the court was rendered by Chief Justice Taney and it contained five important statements: (1) "It was the duty of the executive authority of Ohio upon the demand made by the Governor of Kentucky, and the production of the indictment, duly certified to cause Lago to be delivered up to the agent of the Governor of Kentucky, who was appointed to demand and receive him." (2) "The duty of the Governor of Ohio was merely ministerial, and he had no right to exercise any discretionary power as to the nature or character of the crime charged in the indictment." (3) "The word 'duty' in the act of 1793 means the moral obligation of the state to perform the compact, in the Constitution, when Congress had, by that act, regulated the mode in which the duty should be performed." (4) "But Congress cannot coerce a state officer, as such, to perform any duty by act of Congress. The state officer may perform if he thinks proper, and it may be a moral duty to perform it. But if he refuses, no law of Congress can compel him." (5) "The Governor of Ohio cannot, through the judiciary or any other department of the general government, be compelled to deliver up Lago; and upon that ground only this motion for a mandamus is overruled."[55]

This decision came as a fitting climax to the legal history of the fugitive slave problem as it concerned Kentucky. Such an interpretation placed by the highest judicial authority upon an act of Congress which had stood throughout the slavery era in Kentucky showed beyond any doubt whatever that the legal battle over slavery questions was at an end. If any solution was to be found in the future it would not be in the legislative halls nor in the court room.

[55] 24 Howard's Reports, 109–110.

Emancipation was an important question closely connected with that of the fugitive. This was one of the problems to be discussed in the Constitutional Convention of 1792. There were some few members who were in favor of immediate liberation and others inclined towards a scheme of gradual release of the Negro from bondage. But, as has been shown in the early part of this chapter, the group in favor of the existing institution easily dominated the convention and drew up the famous article IX, which remained without change throughout the slavery era as a part of the fundamental constitutional law. It is significant that it was provided that the legislature should have no power to pass laws for the emancipation of slaves without the consent of their owners, or without paying their owners, previous to such emancipation, a full equivalent in money, for the slaves so emancipated: that the legislature should not pass laws to permit the owners of slaves to emancipate them, saving the rights of creditors, and preventing them from becoming a charge to the counties in which they resided.

From a purely objective viewpoint it is doubtful if a fairer legal guide for the institution of slavery in relation to the rights of emancipation could have been drawn up. On one side, it prevented the State authorities from depriving a slaveholder of his property without due compensation. On the other hand, no unscrupulous master was to free his old and invalid slaves and thereby inflict the burden of their support upon the community as a whole. But this constitutional provision had no legal force in itself. It was to serve as a guide for the enactment of statute laws later.

The State assembly on December 17, 1794, proceeded to the enactment of the first emancipation law of the State. The contents of Article IX of the Constitution were carefully followed and the detailed legal code of emancipation laid down in these words:

It shall be lawful for any person by his or her last will and testament, or by any other instrument in writing, under his or her hand and seal, attested and proved in the county court by two witnesses, or acknowledged by the party in the court of the county where he or she resides, to emancipate or set free his or her slave or slaves: who shall thereupon be entirely and fully discharged from the performance of any contract entered into during servitude, and enjoy as full freedom as if they had been born free. And the said court shall have full power to demand bond and sufficient security of the emancipator, his or her executors or administrators, as the case may be, for the maintenance of any slave or slaves that may be aged or infirm, either of body or mind, to prevent their becoming chargeable to the county. And every slave so emancipated shall have a certificate of freedom from the clerk of such court on parchment with the county seal affixed thereto, for which the clerk shall charge the emancipator five shillings; saving, however, the rights of creditors and every person or persons, bodies politic and corporate, except the heirs or legal representatives of the person so emancipating their slaves.[56]

This law remained throughout the slavery period in Kentucky and the only changes which were ever made in it were in the minor details to untangle some legal ambiguities. The law of 1823, however, is important in showing the discrepancies of the original provisions. By this amendment it was enacted that when the county courts received proof or acknowledgment of a deed of emancipation, or of a will emancipating slaves, they were to note on their record a description of any such slaves. The certificate of freedom which was given to the Negro was also to contain this description and no other certificate was to be issued except on the presentation of proof that the first one had been lost or when such was required for use as evidence in some suit. If any slave thus liberated was found to have presented his certificate to another still held in bondage with a design of freeing him, the emancipated slave was to suffer severe penalties.[57] These added provisions apparently came to fill all the gaps in the previous law and no further amendments of importance were needed to make the laws of emancipation run smoothly.

[56] *Littell's Laws*, 2: 246–247.
[57] Session Laws, 1823, p. 563.

Of all the many slavery cases which were brought before the Court of Appeals in the next thirty years it is interesting to note that nearly all of them concerned themselves more or less with the question of freedom. The very fact that they reached the highest court is also conclusive evidence that the law was not quite as clear as one would at first suppose. Close study of the findings of the court will show that the judiciary was always consistent in its interpretation of the law and that most of the cases were carried up from the lower courts because of disputes between the heirs of an estate and the administrator as to their precedence in the matter of slaves. This part of the controversy concerned itself with the property conception of the slave, whether he was real or personal estate, which was discussed earlier in this chapter. The purely emancipation cases before the Court of Appeals divide themselves into three parts: (1) those which concerned the interpretation of the statute law, (2) those suits for freedom which were based on the question of residence and (3) those which involved persons detained as slaves.

Most of the first class of cases concerned themselves with the emancipation of slaves by will. The number of slaveholders who freed their Negroes during their own lifetime seems to have been very small. On the other hand, from a study of the slave cases in court it appears to have been a very common thing for an owner to provide for the freedom of his slaves in his will. The right of a master to dispose of his own property was beyond dispute, but, as is often the case, the heirs were seldom satisfied and they brought the will into court on one or more technical grounds in an attempt to break the document which freed so much valuable property. The court in every case held that the right of the owner was absolute and that if by the letter of his will his slaves were freed, that right was subject to no dispute. Furthermore, when the Negroes were thus emancipated they did not pass to the personal representatives of the deceased, as assets. They passed by will just as land, and the devise took effect at the death of the testator, whether it be a devise to the slave, of his freedom, or of the slave, to another. The servant, thus affected, had only to appear before the county court and establish his emancipation. This accomplished, it was the duty of the court to give him a certificate of freedom without the consent of the representatives of the emancipator.[58] The right of disposal rested with the owner, who could emancipate by act, or by will, and he who denied the right or placed any claim against it was compelled to show the prohibition.[59]

While the owner had absolute powers of disposal of his own slaves he could not draw up a will of prospective freedom which would hold in spite of the rights of his heirs. If a master desired to be very lenient with his servants, he had to make their freedom absolute and in writing. This was well brought out in the case of an apparently kind-hearted Kentucky slaveholder who provided in his will that his slaves were to select their own master without regard to price. They chose as their future owner a man who did not need them, but who offered to take them at about half their real value. The court held that in such a case the executor was not bound to accept the offer, since the interests of those entitled to the proceeds of the sale, as well as the desire and comfort of the slaves, were to be regarded.[60] Another owner had the right idea, but defeated his own intentions by willing all his forty slaves to the Kentucky Colonization Society. The court held that such an act by no means freed the slaves and that by the laws of the State until they were free they could be hired out and the proceeds considered as a part of the estate.[61]

As in all border States there were many legal battles for freedom, which involved the question of residence on free soil. These cases were largely concerned with the question of the right of a citizen of Kentucky to pass through a free State on business or pleasure attended by his slaves or

[58] Black *vs.* Meaux, 4 Dana, 189.
[59] Susan *vs.* Ladd, 6 Dana, 30.
[60] Hopkins *vs.* Morgan's executor, 3 Dana, 17.
[61] Isaac et al. *vs.* Graves' executor, 16 Ben Monroe, 365.

servants without losing his right of ownership over such slaves. The principle involved was early considered in the Kentucky Court of Appeals and faithfully carried out in succeeding generations, viz.: that a "fixed residence" or being domiciled in a non-slaveholding State would operate to release the slave from the power of the master; but that the transient passing or sojourning therein had no such effect. In an early case in 1820 involving a suit for freedom the court held that a person of color from Kentucky who was permitted to reside in a free State could prosecute his right to freedom in any other State. It was held to be a vested right to freedom, which existed wherever he went.[62] In another instance an owner permitted his slave to go at large for twenty years, but the court held that that alone did not give him freedom. Still under this liberty of movement the slave went off into a free State to reside and the court held that the Negro was then free because his right grew out of the law of the free State and not out of that in which the owner resided.[63] An owner permitted his slave to go to Pennsylvania and remain there for a longer period than six months, with a knowledge of the law passed in that State in 1780, and the Kentucky Court of Appeals held that the slave was entitled to his freedom and that even if the slave had returned to Kentucky his right could be asserted there just as well as in Pennsylvania.[64] But should a slave go with his master to a free State and later return to Kentucky with him, whatever status he had then was to be determined by the law of Kentucky and not by the rule of any State where the slave might have been.[65] The fact that a slave stayed in New York for three months before his return to Kentucky, his owner knowing he was there, and making no effort to bring him away, did not give to such slave a right to freedom.[66] A slaveholder sent one of his

[62] Rankin *vs.* Lydia, 2 A. K. Marshall, 467.
[63] 15 Ben Monroe, 328.
[64] 14 *Ibid.*, 355.
[65] 12 *Ibid.*, 542.
[66] 4 Metcalfe, 231.

The Legal Status of Slavery

servants over into Illinois to cut some wood for a few weeks and later the latter brought suit for freedom on the grounds of residence in a free State but the court denied any such right, since the slave returned to his master in Kentucky voluntarily.[67]

If an emancipated Negro for any reason was held in slavery and later established his right to freedom in court, he could not recover compensation for his services or damages for his detention, unless he could prove that he was held under full knowledge of his right or with good reason to believe him free. If pending his suit for freedom he should be hired out by order of the court, the net hire was to be awarded to him if he succeeded.[68]

The actual number of manumissions which took place in Kentucky will no doubt never be known. Among the few statistics are those of the federal census for 1850 and 1860 and they include only the figures for the one census year. According to this source in 1850 only 152 slaves were voluntarily set free in the State or one slave out of every 1,388, a percentage of only .072; and in 1860 there were 176 Negroes recorded as freed or one out of every 1,281 slaves, a percentage of only .078. We can easily assume from the accounts which we have from papers of that time that these numbers were far short of those that were really set free by their masters. It was the custom of many owners who were about to free their slaves to take them to Cincinnati and there have them set free in the Probate Court.

Early in 1859, forty-nine slaves from Fayette County, mostly women and children, were brought to icinnati and set free and later sent to a colony of emancipated Negroes in Green County, Ohio.[69] In March of the same year Robert Barnet of Lincoln County, Kentucky appeared with eighteen slaves—a father, mother, nine children and three grandchildren and another woman and four boys, who were all emancipated in the Cincinnati Probate Court. Before

[67] 11 Ben Monroe, 210.
[68] 4 Dana, 589, 7 Dana, 360.
[69] *American Anti-Slavery Society Report*, 1859, p. 79.

crossing the Ohio, while in Covington, he was offered $20,-000 for all of them but he stated that he would refuse even $50,000.[70] In January, 1860, William McGinnis, of Bourbon County, appeared with fourteen slaves before the same probate court and set them all free.[71]

The law of Kentucky plainly provided that no slave was to be emancipated unless bond were given that he would immediately leave the State. Hence it was but natural that a master who intended setting his slaves free should take them as slaves to a free State and there give them their freedom, thus satisfying his own conscience and at the same time removing any future legal trouble that might ensue on account of his former slaves being found in the State of Kentucky. For this reason it would seem that a large number of the kind-hearted slaveholders who freed their slaves did so outside the bounds of Kentucky and thus that State was deprived of the credit for many emancipations which took place voluntarily at the hands of her own slaveholders.

[70] *Weekly Free South* (Newport), March 4, 1859.
[71] *American Anti-Slavery Society Report*, 1860, p. 44.

CHAPTER IV

THE SOCIAL STATUS OF THE SLAVE

As many of the slave regulations were enacted to deal with extreme cases and some of them were not generally enforced, it is necessary to consider also the social status of the blacks to determine exactly what the institution was in Kentucky. In this commonwealth slavery was decidedly patriarchal. The slave was not such an unfortunate creature as some have pictured him. He usually had set apart for himself and his family a house which was located near the master's mansion. While this home may have been a rude cabin made of small logs, with a roof covered with splits and an earthern floor, likely as not the master's son was attending school a few weeks in the year in a neighboring log cabin which boasted of no more luxuries than the humble slave dwelling. The servant and his family were well fed and had plenty of domestic cloth for all necessary wearing apparel.

The kind of clothing which the Kentucky slave had can be seen best by a study of the runaway slave advertisements where a description of apparel was often essential to the apprehension of the Negro. "Billy" in 1803 ran away from his owner in Lexington and took such a variety of clothing with him that the master was unable to give a description of them.[1] "Jack," running away from his owner in Mercer County, had on when he left and took with him "one pale blue jeans coat, one gray jeans coat, and an old linsey coat; one pair of cloth pantaloons, one pair of jeans, and one of linen."[2] "Thenton," when leaving his master in Warren County, took with him "a new black smooth fur hat, a yellow woollen jeans frock coat, more than half worn; three

[1] *Lexington Gazette*, August 23, 1803.
[2] *Louisville Public Advertiser*, July 10, 1824.

shirts, two of coarse cotton and one entirely new, the third a bleached domestic and new; one blanket; one pair of pantaloons, of cotton and flax."[3] "Jarret," from Leitchfield, wore when he left "a smooth black Russia hat" and took with him "a pair of buckskin saddle bags . . . and a great deal of clothing, to wit: one brown jeans frock coat, and pantaloons of the same; also, a brown jeans overcoat, with large pockets in the side; a new dark colored overcoat, two pair blue cloth pantaloons, and an old silver watch."[4] The clothing of "Esau," from Meade County, was described as "brown jeans pants, black cassinet pants, blue cloth pants, three fine shirts; one black silk vest and one green vest, one brown jeans frock coat, one pale blue coat, velvet collar; coarse shoes and black hat."[5] "Stewart" left his master in Bullitt County dressed in typical Negro attire— "a black luster coat, made sack fashion, and a pair of snuff colored cassinet pantaloons; also, a black fur hat with low crown and broad brim, and vest with purple dots on it."[6] "George," living in Marion County, had an outfit of "Brown jeans frock coat (skirt lined with home-made flannel dyed with madder), a pair of new black and yellow twilled negro jeans pantaloons, white socks, factory shirt with linen bosom, and black wool hat."[7] An owner advertising in 1852 stated that his slave "Andy" had three suits of clothes with him when he ran away.[8] It is perfectly evident from the reading of these slave advertisements that the male Negroes were as substantially clothed as any members of their race could expect to be at that time even in a state of freedom. The surplus clothing as described above was all a part of the slave's own property and not taken from the master's wardrobe. There were many cases of theft but they need not be considered in this discussion.

A large majority of all runaway slaves were men and

[3] *Louisville Weekly Journal*, October 15, 1845.
[4] *Ibid.*, October 22, 1845.
[5] *Ibid.*, September 27, 1848.
[6] *Ibid.*, May 16, 1849.
[7] *Ibid.*, December 10, 1851.
[8] *Ibid.*, December 22, 1852.

even when advertisements dealt with female fugitives it was only on rare occasions that the owner attempted to give a description of the clothing which was worn. Will Morton in 1806 gave a list of "Letty's" clothing as "two or three white muslin dresses, one of fancy chintz, salmon colored linsey petticoat, white yarn stockings, and good shoes, with sundry other clothing of good quality."[9] At such an early date in the history of Kentucky slavery the apparel of this young slave woman compares very favorably with that which was worn by the white people.

In sickness the slaves were cared for by the same physician who looked after the master and his family and should occasion demand assistance any member of the owner's household might be found nursing a sick Negro. There was no limit to the supply of fuel for the winter, for the slaves had the right to cut timber for their own use anywhere in the woods of the estate.[10]

As in Virginia, the slave was permitted to have a little "truck-patch" of half an acre or more, where he could raise any crop that he desired. In Kentucky these small plots of ground were nearly always filled with sweet potatoes, tobacco and watermelons. The soil was not only conducive to their cultivation but they were the three favorite agricultural products for personal consumption. These particular crops needed little cultivation once they were planted and such as was necessary could easily be done on Saturday afternoons, when the slave was at leisure.

Historians have reminded us that in most of the Southern States there was a tendency for the more energetic of the slaves to work for pay during their idle hours and thus eventually secure a sufficient surplus to buy their own freedom. In Kentucky such cases were very rare. Most Negroes seem to have been content with their condition in such bondage as existed in the State. There were many cases in which a Negro refused to purchase his freedom

[9] *Lexington Gazette,* April 12, 1806.

[10] The best contemporary treatment of this subject in general is by Dr. R. J. Spurr—the sole printed text being in Perrin's *History of Bourbon County,* pp. 59–60.

although he had the necessary amount of money. George Brown, the famous Negro author of *Recollections of an Ex-slave,* published in the *Winchester Democrat,* has given us some experiences which testify to the feeling existing between master and slave. In 1857 his mistress was offered $2,100 for George, but when talking the matter over with him she found that he had serious objections to the prospective purchaser. She showed an interest in Brown's welfare by refusing to sell him. In later years when freedom was within his grasp for the asking, Brown "bought himself" for $1,000 because, as he says in his own words, it was not honorable for him to "swindle his young mistress out of her slave." Such was the example of a Kentucky slave who purchased his own freedom, not for his own benefit, but for that of his mistress.

Another factor entered into this question. In the later years, once a slave secured his liberty, he was immediately required to leave the State and if such a one had lived all his life in Kentucky, he would naturally hesitate to depart into an unknown region. Many of the slaves did earn considerable money by cobbling shoes, cutting wood, and making brooms, but most of them showed little tendency to save their earnings for any future deliverance from bondage. They were more concerned then—as they often are even yet—with the pleasures of the day. More often they were to be found wasting their spare change on whisky, a problem which grew greater for the master with passing years.

In addition to the regular Saturday afternoon and Sunday off every week the slaves were given several other holidays throughout the year, the most extensive being at Christmas time. At Easter they were allowed two or three days rest and when an election was being held there was no work done outside of the regular chores. The general election day in those times was the first Monday in August and it was the custom for most of the slaves throughout the "penny-royal" and "bluegrass" to journey to the county seat, where they would all congregate and have a general frolic in accordance with Negro standards of a good time. In the later years of slavery the towns had established sufficient control of the Negroes gathering in their jurisdiction so that the drink evil was more or less mitigated. The fear of the law was a great incentive to their proper conduct on those rare occasions when they had a whole day in town to themselves without any tasks to perform for their master. As Rothert has well observed, however, the slave sometimes did have to care for his drunken owner and take him home. To the student acquainted with Kentucky history and social conditions such a brief statement suggests a wealth of material on the local type of slavery.

That ardent abolitionist from across the sea, James Silk Buckingham, has recorded a characteristic picture of the Kentucky slave at rest and in gala attire:

"We remained at Henderson the greater part of the day, it being a holiday with the negro slaves on the estate, so that it was difficult to get the requisite number of hands to complete the landing in a short time. Some of the female slaves were very gaily dressed, and many of them in good taste, with white muslin gowns, blue and pink waists, ribbons, silk handkerchiefs or scarfs, straw bonnets, and a reticule for the pocket handkerchief held on the arm. In talking with them, and inquiring the reason of the holiday, one said she believed it was Easter, another said it was Whitsuntide, and a third thought it was midsummer. They were chiefly the household slaves, who are always better treated, better dressed, and more indulgent than the field laborers. The men who were employed in landing the cargo appeared to be more cheerful in their general aspect and behavior than the field slaves I have seen at the South: and there is no doubt that in Kentucky their condition is very much better than in most other states, their work lighter, their food and clothing better, and their treatment more kind and humane."[11]

Legally, there were no marriages among the slaves. They were not citizens, but property. The men were urged to take their "wives" from among the women of the home estate, if a suitable companion could be found. But if not

[11] Buckingham, *Eastern and Western States,* Vol. 3: 41.

they eventually secured one in the neighborhood and the master usually allowed the slave a pass to see his wife every night in the week. While such a cohabitation was not exactly a legal affair most of them were held as sacred as those more legalized unions among the master class. Many masters paid an unconscious tribute to these unions. When there ran away a slave who had a wife living in the neighborhood or even at a great distance the owner would make mention of the exact locality of the wife in order that people in that region would be on the lookout for the fugitive. J. C. Bucklin in 1824 did not give much of a description of David, who had left his master, but he very carefully stated that he had a "wife and children at William Shirley's, about 16 miles from this place, on the Westport Road."[12] An owner in Fayette county after giving a detailed picture of "Arthur" added that "Capt. Peter Poindexter, eight miles from Lexington owns his wife, and I expect that he will be in that neighborhood."[13] A more extreme example was that of "Dick," a Lexington slave who ran away to New Orleans, the owner thought, because "he has a wife living in that city, and he has been heard to say frequently that he was determined to go to New Orleans."[14] Such cases as this were the logical consequence of the slavery system. They existed in Kentucky just as in any other slave State, but they were few compared with those slaves unions that were never broken.

It was to the economic as well as humanitarian interest of the master to have sympathy with the peace and contentment of his servant. Thus most of them took care that the family relationships of the slaves should not be disturbed. Oftentimes when the owner of either a husband or a wife was on the point of moving out of the county the masters would get together and make a trade which would obviate any disruption of the slave family. Under such conditions a man would part with a servant who otherwise could not

[12] *Louisville Public Advertiser*, August 11, 1824.
[13] *Lexington Gazette*, June 14, 1803.
[14] *Lexington Intelligencer*, July 7, 1838.

have been bought at any price. Such a situation was possible only in a State where the personal interest in a slave and his welfare took precedence over merely his economic value to the owner.[15]

Charles Stewart in *My Life as a Slave* has given us his own experiences of home life and marriage among slaves in Kentucky. He lived in Paris and was engaged in handling race horses. Soon after coming from Virginia to Kentucky he fell in love with a young mulatto girl, who was the property of a Mr. Robertson, who gave his consent to their marriage, promising never to part them by his own free will. In his own dialect Stewart dictated his story. "So I married her, an' tuk her to a little house I had fixed up near de stables, an' she clear-starched an' sewed an' 'broidered an' wukked wid de hand-loom, an' made more pretty things dan I could count. She paid her marster, en course, reg'lar, so much a month fur her hire, but, lor', she neber touched her airnin's fur dat. I had plenty of money to hire as many wives as I wanted, but dis one was de onliest one I eber did want, an' so it was easy enough." After two years his wife became very sick and died and the grief of the Negro man was touching in the extreme. "She was jes' as fond o' me as I was of her, an' it did 'pear hard luck to lose her jes' as I was makin' up my mind to buy her out and out, only en course, it was a fortunate thing I hadn't bought her, as long as she had to die, kase den I would ha' lost her an' de money too. Arter she was in de ground it jes' 'peared to me like eberything was different; I tuk a dislikement to Paris, an' I didn't feel like goin' home to Virginny." His master agreed to let him go wherever he liked if he could find an owner to suit him and finally Stewart went to Louisiana after an interview with Senator Porter of that State. He was to stay six months to see how he liked it and then if agreeable he was to stay there. He must have been a rather unusual Negro, for his selling price was finally fixed at $3,500.[16]

[15] Perrin (Bourbon County), p. 60.
[16] *Harper's Magazine*, October, 1884, pp. 730–738.

But life among the slaves of Kentucky was not by any means a path of roses. Many anti-slavery leaders attested to this fact. The most trustworthy statement that was ever made on this general subject was that embodied in the pamphlet of the Presbyterian Synod of Kentucky in 1835 advocating gradual emancipation. The following brief extracts are most significant:

"The system produces general licentiousness among the slaves. Marriage, as a civil ordinance, they cannot enjoy. Until slavery waxeth old, and tendeth to decay, there cannot be any legal recognition of the marriage rite, or the enforcement of its consequent duties. For, all the regulations on this subject would limit the master's absolute right of property in the slaves. In his disposal of them he could no longer be at liberty to consult merely his own interest . . . their present quasi-marriages are continually voided (at the master's pleasure). . . . They are in this way brought to consider their matrimonial alliances as things not binding, and act accordingly. We are then assured by the most unquestionable testimony that licentiousness is the necessary result of our system.

One would infer from this observation of apparently fair-minded men that slave unions were not very sacred affairs and that any disruption of them would amount to little, but in the same document these Presbyterian preachers give a back-handed compliment to the stability, at least in temperament, of the average slave marriage.

"Brothers and sisters, parents and children, husbands and wives, are torn asunder and permitted to see each other no more. These acts are daily occurring in the midst of us. The shrieks and agony often witnessed on such occasions proclaim with a trumpet tongue, the iniquity of our system. There is not a neighborhood where these heartrending scenes are not displayed; there is not a village or road that does not behold the sad procession of manacled outcasts, whose mournful countenances tell that they are exiled by force, from all that their hearts hold dear."

It is strange that these two opposing views should appear in the same pamphlet, but nevertheless they are both undoubtedly true pictures of slavery in Kentucky. It is merely a question as to which of the two represented the majority of cases. Licentiousness there was, but it was certainly very much less among the slaves of Kentucky than in the far South. Slave unions were treated with more respect by the masters of Kentucky than in most slave States. As has been pointed out in a previous chapter, the very fact that the few instances of inhuman separation of slave families produced such a storm of public disapproval shows that it was not a very general practice in the State.

From the legal standpoint the slave had no rights or privileges in the attainment of even a meager education. On the other hand Kentucky was the only slave State, with the exception of Maryland and Tennessee, which never passed any laws forbidding the instruction of slaves. Thus no penalty was attached to Negro education, neither was any encouragement given. Those slaves who learned to read were the servants of masters who because of conscientious scruples taught them how to read the Bible. Few slaves ever learned to write, for they might then be tempted to serve as unofficial dispensers of passes in the owner's name. The general objection to any reasonable amount of education was the tendency towards dissatisfaction with the servile status thereby aroused. If the slave could learn to read well, it was feared that he would become a victim of the "filthy" abolitionist literature, which through the resultant effect upon the Negroes would have produced no end of trouble to the slavery system. Hence, for the most part, the Kentucky slave remained in blissful ignorance, and well for him as such and the institution he represented that his learning was no greater.[17]

Out of a collection of some three hundred and fifty runaway slave advertisements concerning Kentucky slaves the author has found 71 cases in which mention was made that the Negro could read and 37 instances in which he could write. The latter cases are all included in the former

[17] Clarke, *Sufferings of Lewis and Milton Clarke*, p. 104.
Rothert, *History of Muhlenburg County*, p. 104.
Perrin (Bourbon County), p. 60.

classification also. On that basis a little over ten per cent of the slaves could read and write and about twenty per cent could read but were unable to write. There are, however, two strong reasons against any such general conclusion. In the first place, the more a slave learned the more liable he was to become dissatisfied and run away; and secondly, the careful mention which was made in advertisements of the Negro's ability to read or write would tend to show that it was more or less an unusual accomplishment.

Taking up the question of the education of slaves in the State, the Presbyterian Synod of Kentucky said in 1834 that "Slavery dooms thousands of human beings to hopeless ignorance . . . if slaves are educated it must involve some outlay upon the part of the master. . . . It is inconsistent with our knowledge of human nature to suppose that he will do this for them. The present state of instruction among this race remains exactly what we might . . . naturally anticipate. Throughout the whole land (State), so far as we can learn, there is but one school in which, during the week, slaves can be taught. The light of three or four Sabbath schools is seen glimmering through the darkness that covers the black population of the whole State. Here and there a family is found where humanity and religion impel the master, mistress or children to the laborious task of private instruction."[18]

It should be added in this connection that the same statement would hold true of the free Negro population of Kentucky at the same period. Until long after the Civil War there was no provision made for their education other than that of individual enterprise. The public education of the whites was not on a plane comparable to that of any of the Northern States until after the reconstruction period, and even then Kentucky lagged behind for years.

The church and its influence for the betterment of society under the slavery system was more effective than the school. The chief religious paper of the State was the *Presbyterian Herald* and one of its most persistent pleas was that the

[18] *Address to the People of Kentucky*, p. 8.

proper religious instruction of the Negro servant class would answer most of the objections to the institution. "The most formidable weapon in the hands of the abolitionist," said the editor, "is the indifference which he charges to the Christian slaveholder toward the spiritual welfare of the slave under his control. Disarm him of this weapon, and you have done much to render him powerless."[19]

Religious instruction in families of Christian habits of life, however, was not so sadly neglected. The household servants were usually brought to the house during the family worship and the scriptures were not merely read to them but explained. No restrictions were ever placed on church attendance either by law or by custom. Many slaves united with the white churches and throughout the State today one may find any number of old churches whose records still show several of these Negroes on the church rolls. Most of them are very kindly remembered for their good moral character and abiding faith. Such a condition was not so prevalent among the agricultural slaves, except where they were few in numbers. Even here, however, the religious instinct was not suppressed in any manner. Their religion at the most was a very crude imitation of the worship of their masters. They were not confined to the rear seats of the white churches for their attendance at Sunday services. They could hold their own meetings in schoolhouses and vacant church edifices.

It was these distinctively slave gatherings that gave rise to one of the most interesting of all Negro characters—the preacher. Tradition and story have related many a charming picture of this quaint representative of Negro faith, but unfortunately few life stories of any of them have ever been preserved. In nearly all the county histories we find mention of several of these Negro exhorters who seemingly were men of some degree of intelligence. The majority of them were apparently themselves slaves, subject to the will

[19] *Presbyterian Herald*, April 16, 1846. See especially the editorial and articles in the issue of October 4, 1849.

of their masters, and while the restrictions on their movements were very lax, they seldom if ever spoke beyond the borders of their home county.[20]

One of the famous Negro preachers of the early nineteenth-century South was Josiah Henson. From 1825 to 1828 he was a slave in Daviess County, Kentucky, and in his autobiography he has given us a picture of the circumstances under which he became a slave preacher. "In Kentucky," said he, "the opportunities of attending on the preaching of whites, as well as of blacks, were more numerous; and partly attended by them, and the campmeetings which occurred from time to time, and partly from studying carefully my own heart, and observing the developments of character around me, in all the stations of life which I could watch, I became better acquainted with those religious feelings which are deeply implanted in the breast of every human being, and learnt by practice how best to arouse them, and keep them excited, and in general to produce some good religious impressions on the ignorant and thoughtless community by which I was surrounded. . . . I cannot but derive some satisfaction, too, from the proofs I have had that my services have been acceptable to those to whom they have been rendered. In the course of the three years from 1825 to 1828 I availed myself of all the opportunities of improvement which occurred and was admitted as a preacher by a conference of the Methodist Episcopal Church."[21]

In Ballard County there was another interesting exhorter. Advertising for his Negro Jack who had run away in 1850, C. B. Young pointed out that although he was a slave and the property of the "subscriber" he was a well-educated Baptist preacher and in the pursuit of his vocation he was well known by "many of the citizens of Paducah, McCracken County, and also by citizens of Hickman and Fulton Counties, and is thought by many to be a free man."[22]

[20] Rothert, *History of Muhlenburg County*, p. 340.
[21] Henson, *Life of Josiah Henson*, pp. 26–27.
[22] *Louisville Weekly Journal*, March 27, 1850.

The only credentials which the Negro preacher carried, according to his own testimony, came directly from the Lord. His education was only of a sufficient character to enable him to read the Bible and line out the words of the hymns. His creed was never the creation of any school of theology. It was usually an original interpretation of supernatural phenomena varying widely even in one individual from time to time. Convinced of his supernatural calling, he felt inferior to no one in the power of exegesis. As long as he held his balance and remained on terra firma his followers believed in him as he believed in himself. But as Lucius Little has well said: "Once in a while a colored preacher lost his influence with his congregation by drinking too deeply of the Pierian spring. Too much learning raised him out of their orbit. They fell on stony ground." Strange, yet how true, that the more ignorant a slave minister was, the more power of influence for good he had among his fellow human beings.[23]

James Lane Allen has given us a splendid little sketch of three of these native characters whom he evidently knew in his younger days:

"One of these negro preachers was allowed by his master to fill a distant appointment. Belated once, and returning home after the hour forbidden for slaves to be abroad, he was caught by the patrol and cruelly whipped. As the blows fell, his words were, "Jesus Christ suffered for righteousness' sake; so kin I."

Another was recommended for deacon's orders and actually ordained. When liberty came, he refused to be free, and continued to work in his master's family until his death. With considerable knowledge of the Bible and a fluent tongue, he would nevertheless sometimes grow confused while preaching and lose his train of thought. At these embarrassing junctures it was his wont suddenly to call out at the top of his voice, "Saul, Saul. Why persecutest thou me?" The effect upon his hearers was electrifying: —as none but a very highly favored being could be thought worthy of enjoying this persecution. He thus converted his loss of mind into spiritual reputation.

[23] Little, L. P., *Ben Hardin, his Times and Contemporaries*, pp. 544–545.

A third named Peter Cotton, united the vocations of exhorter and wood-chopper. He united them literally, for one moment Peter might be seen standing on his log chopping away, and the next kneeling down beside it praying. He got his mistress to make him a long jeans coat and on the ample tails of it to embroider, by his direction, sundry texts of scripture, such as " Come unto Me, all ye that are heavy laden." Thus literally clothed with righteousness, Peter went from cabin to cabin, preaching the Word. Well for him if that other Peter could have seen him.''[24]

One of the dominant features of such a type of religion among the Negroes was the resulting prevalence of superstition. It almost seems that in their ignorance they adopted every form of supernatural fear that was ever known among our ancestors. But if it had ended there the matter would not have been so important socially. In their constant association with white children they brought their fears of "ghost-hauntings" and other fantastic ideas into the minds of the very young. The peculiarity of the Negro slave as compared with the other superstitious races was his own sinister imaginative productions. They related none of the valuable tales of ancient mythology, but rather did they fill the earth with goblins, witches and ghosts—the result of their own dreams and fancies.[25]

The many stories of this sort which a "mammy" related to a child a half century ago can be reproduced by the old man of the twentieth century and the effect of the old ideas of magic is still with him. The prevalence of superstitious ideas in Kentucky today might easily be traced back to the associations of slavery times. But such a weakness may not always have done harm; not every child was so influenced. The natural play of the Negro instinct was worth much to his peace and contentment. Here again Shaler has given us a rather unique observation from his own experience:

[24] Allen, James Lane, *Blue Grass Region of Kentucky*, pp. 77–78.
[25] Robertson's *Autobiography*, pp. 124–125.

"The only movements of the spirit in the religious field that I can remember came from two sources: my mother's singing. . . . The other spiritual influence came from the negroes. A number of them used to meet at night to talk religion beneath a shed which lay open to the northern sky. One of them, well named "Old Daniel," had a fervid imagination and excellent descriptive powers. He would picture the coming of the great angel as if it were before his eyes; the path of light shooting down from about the North star,—the majesty of his train. Then the rolling of the heavens "like a scroll"—I did not know what this process was like, but it seemed vaguely fine—and then the burning up of the world. I was always greatly moved when hearing these exhortations which must indeed have been rather wonderful things, but they made no permanent impression upon me. In fact I regarded them as ' nigger talk.' "[26]

The patriarchal character of slavery as it existed in Kentucky is best shown in the relationship which generally existed between the master and his slave. The pioneers who brought their slaves with them from Virginia encountered many dangers not only in crossing the mountains but after they had settled in the new State. Many were the times when the slave proved himself a hero and even encountered death in order to protect the master and his family. Tradition and history have handed down many of these stories to us, but the most famous of all, as well as the best authenticated, was the experience of Monk Estill, who was the slave of Colonel James Estill, of Madison County. In a struggle with the Indians in 1782 in the region where Mount Sterling is now located Monk cried out to his master in the thick of the fray: "Don't give way, Marse Jim; there's only twenty-five of the Injuns and you can whip them." Colonel Estill was killed and Monk was taken prisoner but he soon managed to escape, and after joining his comrades carried one of the wounded men twenty-five miles. The young master was so grateful to Monk that he gave him his freedom and kept him in the best of comfort the rest of his life. This was the experi-

[26] Shaler's *Autobiography*, pp. 57–58.

ence of what is supposed to have been the first slave in the district of Kentucky.[27]

Not only was the slave on a par with his master when it came to facing dangers but even in the field of sports he had as pleasant an outing as his overlord. While the one may have spent the day in fox hunting or deer driving, when nightfall came the Negro was apt to emerge from his quarters followed by his faithful dog in search of possum or coon. While the master may have enjoyed a feast of venison at his table the Negro was just as well satisfied with the less valuable but savory game that graced his own meal.

With the exception of the house servants most of the slaves of the State were employed in agricultural pursuits, but, as we have seen elsewhere, even here they were not to be found in large droves as in the States of the South. There were only a few big landed estates which were cultivated by the owners under their own supervision and in the large majority of cases the field slaves worked side by side with the whites. Often an owner's circumstances compelled him to labor in the fields with his slaves and when doing so he rarely demanded more of them than he did himself. Such a condition was not only true in the early days when there were few slaves but it extended throughout the slavery era.[28] The stories of the mildness of the institution in Kentucky which reached the North were little accredited by the radical element, which could never see any virtue in servile labor. Perhaps the most zealous abolitionist who visited the State was J. W. Buckingham, who wrote in 1840 that the "condition of the Negroes, as to food, clothing, and light labor struck me as being better in Kentucky than in any other State."[29] While traveling in the heart of the slave section of the State between Frankfort and Louisville he saw many instances of black and white laborers, slave and free, working side by side in the same field.[30]

[27] Collins, *History of Kentucky*, Vol. 2, pp. 634–636.
[28] Cotterill, *History of Pioneer Kentucky*, p. 245.
Little, L. P., *Ben Hardin, his Times and Contemporaries*, p. 543.
[29] Buckingham, *Eastern and Western States*, Vol. 3: 7–8.
[30] *Op. cit.*, Vol. 3: 8.

The relation between the owner and the household type of slave was of a more intimate nature and the master was careful to pick only the best of the Negroes. In such an environment we see the picture of the Kentucky gentleman of song and story, and the Negro in all the best that tradition has related of him. The latter became identified with the family of the master in sentiment and feeling. Under ordinary circumstances he had nothing to worry about, and with no cares pressing upon him, he became as happy as any Negro ever was. If the crops failed, or the owner became bankrupt he had none of the anxiety of his master, although he may have displayed the greatest sympathy with the existing condition. It was his duty to give only his labor to his master and in return he was sheltered, clothed and supported when sick or too old to labor; and at last when his earthly toils were over, he was given a Christian burial. The humble affection which the slave had for his master in conjunction with the extreme confidence which he held for the outcome of all pecuniary troubles is shown by instances in the life history of every slaveholding family. No matter what might be the circumstances and conditions of the estate the slave could go on in his daily work without any fears or cares, except for the one great cloud that in the event of a disruption of the estate through a legal process he might be sold to satisfy his master's creditors.

From our present viewpoint the treatment may have been at times rather harsh but we must be careful to judge it from the general standard of those times. It has been pointed out that it would bear "favorable comparison with the treatment of the white sailors in the British and American navies of the same period."[31] The slave code allowed a much severer policy than was generally carried out, for it must be considered that the law was made to fit the worst cases, where such action was justifiable. Often the attitude of the master appeared harsher than it was really meant to be. It may have been merely a display of authority on his

[31] Little, L. P., *Ben Hardin, his Times and Contemporaries*, pp. 541-2.

part when he reprimanded a servant who had really committed only a minor indiscretion.[32]

There were naturally other scenes in which the treatment of slaves would not appear in such a favorable light. The chronically bad master, however, was at all times and under all circumstances under the ban of a just public sentiment. Should, by chance, a slave under such a one secure vengeance on his heartless overlord, the general feeling of the community was on the side of the slave. Strange to say, it was very often true that persons who had known little concerning slavery until they came to Kentucky, as soon as they had accumulated a sufficient surplus, became the owners of slaves and proved to be the hardest taskmasters.[33] Much light is thrown on this situation by Shaler.

[32] A typical example of this has been related by one of Kentucky's distinguished sons:

"In the households where I was intimate the slaves were about on the same footing as the other members of the family; they were subjected to sudden explosions of the master's temper much as were his children. I well remember a frequent scene in my grandfather's house, where it was the custom that I should go every Sunday afternoon for counsel and instruction. They were at first somewhat fearsome occasions for a little lad thus to be alone with an aged and stately grandfather. I soon won his interest, in some measure by my fears, and came greatly to enjoy the intercourse, for he knew how to talk to a boy, and we became, in a way, boys together, in our sense of the funny side of things. It was the custom, too, for him to divide the session of three or four hours with a brief nap taken in his chair. . . .

"As his rooms were near the negro quarter he would make ready for his siesta by sending forth the servantman who waited on him, bidding him tell the people that they were to keep quiet during the performance. I can see him now with his pig-tail hanging down behind the back of the easy chair and a handkerchief over his face as he courted slumber. For a minute or two it would be still, then the hidden varlets would be as noisy as before. Then the pig-tail would begin to twitch, and he would mutter: 'Jim, tell those people they *must* be still.' Again a minute of quiet, and once more the jabbering and shouting. Now with a leap he would clutch his long walking-stick and charge the crowd in the quarter, laying about him with amazing nimbleness, until all the offenders were run to their holes. Back he would come from his excursion and settle himself to sleep. I could see that his rage was merely on the surface and that he had used it for a corrective, for he evidently took care not to hurt anyone." Shaler's *Autobiography*, p. 37.

[33] Little, L. P., *Ben Hardin, his Times and Contemporaries*, p. 543.

"There is a common opinion," said he, "that the slaves of the Southern households were subjected in various ways to brutal treatment. Such, in my experience, was not the case. Though the custom of using the whip on white children was common enough, I never saw a negro deliberately punished in that way until 1862, when, in military service, I stayed at night at the house of a friend. This old man, long a widower, had recently married a woman from the state of Maine, who had been the governess of his children. In the early morning I heard a tumult in the back yard, and on looking out saw a negro man, his arms tied up to a limb of a tree, while the vigorous matron was administering on his back with a cowhide whip. At breakfast I learned that the man had well deserved the flogging, but it struck me as curious that in the only instance of the kind that I had known the punishment was from the hands of a Northern woman."[34] Shaler lived in Campbell County in the extreme northern section of the State, where there were only a few slaves and the treatment was milder perhaps than in any other part of Kentucky.

The general attitude is best shown by the two laws passed in 1816 and 1830. It had always been considered that the slave, being the property of his owner, it remained for him and for him alone to serve as the disciplinarian of the Negro. The increasing abuse of this right by outsiders led to a law in 1815 giving the owners a power of action against persons abusing their slaves, and in February, 1816, the provisions were made more specific. If any person should "whip, strike or otherwise abuse the slave of another" without the owner's consent, the latter could recover damages in any circuit court in the commonwealth—regardless of whether or not the punishment so inflicted injured the ability of the slave to render service to his master.[35]

Some of the contemporary comment would seem to imply that the theory of the law was based on the property con-

[34] Shaler's *Autobiography*, pp. 36–37.
[35] *Littell's Laws*, Vol. 5: 578–579.

ception of the slave and not upon humanitarian motives. In other words, it was perfectly proper to punish any slave as one saw fit as long as one did not interfere with the property value of the servant. Fearon, while visiting the State in 1818, came across an example of this kind and after telling the story of the punishment makes this comment: "It appears that this boy (the one who had been whipped) was the property of a regular slave-dealer, who was then absent at Natchez with a cargo. Mr. Lawe's humanity fell lamentably in my estimation when he stated, that 'whipping niggers, if they were his own, was perfectly right, and they perhaps deserved it; but what made him mad was, that the boy was left under his care by a friend, and he did not like to have a friend's property injured.' "[36] The conduct observed by Fearon was clearly in violation of the law of 1816, unless the absent master had given over his rights in full to the man Lawe, who administered the punishment. It may have been the spirit of the laws of Kentucky that Lawe had in mind when he spoke to Fearon. On the other hand, it could easily be given the interpretation which Fearon made. The trend of public opinion was more and more in the interest of justice for the slave as the law of 1830 shows:

> If any owner of a slave shall treat such slave cruelly, so as in the opinion of the jury, to endanger the life or limb of such slave, or shall not supply his slave with sufficient food or raiment, it shall and may be lawful for any person acquainted with the fact or facts, to state and set forth in a petition to the Circuit Court, the facts, or any of them aforesaid, of which the defendant hath been guilty, and pray that such slave or slaves may be taken from the possession of the owner, and sold for the benefit of such owner, agreeably to the 7th article of the Constitution.[37]

In accordance with this law, if a jury of twelve men were convinced that a master treated his slave cruelly, or failed to provide him the proper food and clothing, the

[36] Fearon, *Sketches in America*, p. 241.
[37] Session Laws, 1830, p. 174.

slave would be sold into better hands and the master would have to pay the costs of the suit. Most assuredly there was no place in the eyes of the law for an inhuman slaveholder. Not only was such a one a criminal in the eyes of the courts but he was socially ostracized in the ordinary circles of the community.[38]

Two instances of this kind in Lexington will show the public feeling. In 1837 Mrs. Turner, the wife of a wealthy Lexington judge, was accused of inhuman cruelty. Her own husband was the chief complainant, stating that "that woman has been the cause of the death of six of my servants by her severities." The trial caused intense excitement among the people of Lexington, more so perhaps for the reason that the defendant was a member of a prominent Boston family and her husband was a former judge of the criminal court in New Orleans. The court proceedings were brought to an end when the woman was pronounced insane and placed in the asylum.[39]

Early in 1839 a Mr. and Mrs. Maxwell were tried in Lexington for the inhuman treatment of a female slave servant. The indignation of the citizens of Lexington is apparent from the publicity that was given to the proceedings in the local papers. A Dr. Constant testified that he saw Mrs. Maxwell whipping the Negro severely, without being particular whether she struck her in the face or not. The lacerations had brought blood in considerable quantities for he had found some on the steps. He had noticed previously that the slave had been thinly clad and was barefooted even in cold weather. During the previous months he had noticed several scars on her and at one time she had had one eye tied up for a week. A Mr. Winters was once passing along the street and saw one of the boys whipping the slave girl with a cowhide. Whenever she turned her face to him he would hit her across the face either with the butt end or small end of the whip to make her turn around square to the lash, in order that he might get a fair blow at her. A Mr.

[38] Blanchard and Rice, *Debate on Slavery*, p. 135.
[39] *American Slavery As It Is*, p. 87.

Say had noticed several wounds on her person, chiefly bruises. Capt. Porter, the keeper of the workhouse, thought the injuries on Milly's person were very bad, some of them appeared to be burns, and some were bruises or stripes from a cowhide whip. The trial was held amidst a turmoil of resentment against the defendants and there was apparently no one in sympathy with them whatever.[40]

Any discussion of the relationships in slavery times would be incomplete without adding the characterization of the Kentucky master as drawn by a celebrated author who was born in the heart of the bluegrass and was thoroughly familiar with the type:

"The good in nature is irrepressible. Slavery, evil as it was, when looked at from the remoteness of human history as it is to be, will be judged an institution that gave development to a certain noble type of character.

"Along with other social forces peculiar to the age, it produced in Kentucky a kind of farmer the like of which will never appear again. He had the aristocratic virtues: highest notions of personal liberty and personal honor, a fine especial scorn of anything that was little, mean, cowardly. As an agriculturist he was not driving or merciless or grasping; the rapid amassing of wealth was not among his passions, the contention of splendid living not among his thorns. To a certain carelessness of riches he added a certain profuseness of expenditure; and indulgent towards his own pleasures, towards others, his equals or dependents, he bore himself with a spirit of kindness and magnanimity. Intolerant of tyranny, he was no tyrant. To say of such a man, as Jefferson said of every slave-holder, that he lived in the perpetual exercise of the most boisterous passions and unremitting despotism, and in the exaction of the most degrading submission, was to pronounce judgment hasty and unfair.

"Rather did Mrs. Stowe, while not blind to his faults, discern his virtues when she made him, embarrassed by death, exclaim: "If anybody had said to me that I should sell Tom down south to one of those rascally traders, I should have said, 'Is thy servant a dog that he should do this thing?' "[41]

[40] *Lexington Reporter*, January 15, 1839.
[41] Allen, James Lane, *Blue Grass Region of Kentucky*, pp. 67–68.

CHAPTER V

Public Opinion Regarding Emancipation and Colonization

Although the facts herein set forth indicate that slavery in Kentucky was a comparatively mild form of servitude it is not the aim here to leave the impression that the anti-slavery element found no grounds for attacking the institution. On the contrary, there were various elements that devised schemes for exterminating the institution. This was especially true of the churches, which represented more than any other one force the sentiment of the State on the subject of emancipation. The three prominent Protestant denominations of the State were the Presbyterians, the Baptists, and the Methodists. The only one of the three which maintained a general continuous policy throughout the early nineteenth century on the question of slavery was the Presbyterian.

It was on the eve of the first Constitutional Convention of 1792 that David Rice, at that time the leader of the Presbyterians in Kentucky, published a pamphlet under the nom-de-plume of PHILANTHROPOS entitled *Slavery Inconsistent with Justice and Good Policy*. While the author went into the general evils of slavery, such as the lack of protection to female chastity, lack of religious and moral instruction, and the comparative unproductiveness of slave labor, he was not one of those violent opponents of the institution, who would abolish the whole system without any constructive measures. A large part of his treatise was devoted to the supposed sanction of the scriptures and his own evidence that the same source was against rather than in favor of the system then in vogue. It was but natural that Rice should recommend that the convention should put an end to slavery in Kentucky in view of his firm opinions in the matter, but he had a clear vision of the future and he expressed his conviction that "a gradual emancipation only can be advisable." He summed up his ideas in this sentence: "The legislature, if they judged it expedient, would prevent the importation of any more slaves; they would enact that all born after such a date should be free; be qualified by proper education to make useful citizens, and be actually freed at a proper age."[1] He put these ideas forth as a citizen of Kentucky who was interested in its welfare and as a prospective member of the constitutional convention. When that body assembled at Danville he did not hesitate to voice his views again but the forces of slavery were dominant and the majority enacted the famous article IX, which determined the slave code of the State until the institution was abolished by the 13th amendment to the federal constitution. The significance of the attitude of David Rice lies in the fact that as early as the year 1792 he put forth the idea of gradual emancipation, a policy far in advance of his age but which in the course of time was held by a large number of the fair-minded statesmen of Kentucky.

In 1794 the Transylvania Presbytery, which was the governing body of that sect at that time for the whole State, passed a resolution asking that slaves should be instructed to read the Bible, having in view the sole idea that when freedom did come to them they would be prepared for it.[2] The same body in 1796 expressed the following fair-minded attitude in the form of a resolution:

> Although the Presbytery are fully convinced of the great evil of slavery, yet they view the final remedy as alone belonging to the civil powers; and also do not think that they have sufficient authority from the word of God to make it a term of Christian communion. They, therefore, leave it to the consciences of the brethren to act as they may think proper; earnestly recommending to the people under their care to emancipate such of their slaves as they may think fit subjects of liberty; and that they also take every possible measure, by teaching their young slaves to read and give them such other instruction as may be in their power, to prepare

[1] Davidson, *History of the Presbyterian Church in Kentucky*, p. 336.
[2] *Minutes of Transylvania Presbytery*, Vol. 1, p. 147.

them for the enjoyment of liberty, an event which they contemplate with the greatest pleasure, and which, they hope, will be accomplished as soon as the nature of things will admit.[3]

In the year 1797 the same organization decided that slavery was a moral evil but on the question of whether those persons holding slaves were guilty of a moral evil they decided in the negative. As to what persons were guilty they were unable to decide and the matter was postponed for future action.[4]

As early as 1800 the West Lexington Presbytery pointed to the trouble and division which slavery was likely to cause among the churches, but they were unable to come to any decision upon the exclusion of slaveholding members from church privileges and in a letter to the Synod of Virginia they asked for the judgment of higher ecclesiastical authorities.[5] In 1802 the same body decided on a policy of noninterference with the rights of the slaveholding members of the church.[6]

Beginning in 1823 the Synod of Kentucky advocated the cause of the American Colonization Society. Their general attitude on the slavery question was an open one as late as the year 1833 when they adopted a resolution to the effect that "inasmuch as in the judgment of the Synod it is inexpedient to come to any decision on the very difficult and delicate question of slavery as it is within our bounds; therefore, resolved, that the whole matter be indefinitely postponed."[7] The vote on this resolution stood 41 to 36.

The enactment of the law of 1833 forbidding the importation of slaves into Kentucky seems to have induced the Synod to take a step in advance, for when they next met in 1834 at Danville they adopted by the decisive vote of 56 to 7 a resolution calling for the appointment of a committee of ten to draw up a plan for the instruction and future emanci-

[3] *Minutes of Transylvania Presbytery*, Vol. 2, pp. 102–3.
[4] *Ibid.*, Vol. 2, pp. 163, 224.
[5] *Minutes W. Lexington Presbytery*, Vol. 1, p. 38.
[6] *Ibid.*, p. 81.
[7] *Minutes of Kentucky Synod*, Vol. 5, pp. 28, 31.

pation of slaves in the State.[8] The following year this committee published a 64-page pamphlet entitled "An Address to the Presbyterians of Kentucky proposing a plan for the instruction and emancipation of their slaves." Many editions of this work were published throughout the country even as late as 1862 when it was issued by the United Presbyterian Board of Publication in Pittsburgh. It was heralded throughout the northern section of the United States as a very able document and was regarded all the more valuable because it was published in a slaveholding State. The major portion of the pamphlet was taken up with the general arguments setting forth the evils of the slavery system but in the last few pages they set down their plan for the gradual emancipation of the slaves in Kentucky—the most able contribution towards a reconstruction of the existing social system in the State which had been made up to that time.

"The plan, then, which we propose is, for the master to retain during a limited period, and with regard to the welfare of the slave, that authority which he before held, in perpetuity, and solely for his own interest. Let the full liberty of the slave be secured against all contingencies, by a recorded deed of emancipation, to take effect at a specified time. In the meanwhile, let the servant be treated with kindness—let all those things which degrade him be removed—let him enjoy means of instruction, let his moral and religious improvement be sought—let his prospects be presented before him, to stimulate him to acquire those habits of foresight, economy, industry, activity, skill and integrity, which will fit him for using well the liberty he is soon to enjoy." The actual plan of potential freedom was stated briefly in these words: "(1) We would recommend that all slaves now under 20 years of age, and all those yet to be born in our possession, be emancipated as they severally reach their 25th year. (2) We recommend that deeds of emancipation be drawn up, and recorded in our respective county courts, specifying the slaves whom we are about

[8] *Minutes of Kentucky Synod*, Vol. 5, pp. 50–52.

to emancipate, and the age at which each is to be free. (3) We recommend that our slaves be instructed in the common elementary branches of education. (4) We recommend that strenuous and persevering efforts be made to induce them to attend upon the ordinary services of religion, both domestic and public. (5) We recommend that great pains be taken to teach them the Holy Scriptures; and that, to effect this the instrumentality of Sabbath Schools, wherever they can be enjoyed, be united with that of domestic instruction."[9]

This appeal was not to the officials of the State but to the members of a particular religious body by its governing organization. The success or failure of the plan depended entirely upon the individual slaveholder's attitude in the matter. The committee added this sentence by way of explanation: "These are measures which all ought to adopt; and we know of no peculiarity of circumstances in the case of any individual which can free him from culpability if he neglects them."[10]

The sentiments embodied in this appeal were not, however, any indication of the feeling among the slaveholding Presbyterians of the State nor were they expressive of the Synod itself, for that body never took any action upon the address, it being the work of the committee of ten entirely.[11] Davidson, writing in 1847, made the following comment on the sentiment of the church people in Kentucky at that time. "In the morbid and feverish state of the public mind, it is not to be concealed, that by some they (the Committee) were considered as going to an unwarrantable and imprudent length. The northern abolitionists were waging a hot crusade against slavery, sending out itinerant lecturers, and loading the mails with inflammatory publications. Their measures were marked with a fanatical virulence rarely exhibited, and the people were exasperated beyond forbearance ... the effects were truly disastrous. The prospect of emancipation was retarded for years. The laws bearing on the slave population were made more stringent than ever,

[9] *Address to Presbyterians of Kentucky*, pp. 33–34.
[10] *Ibid.*, p. 34.
[11] Davidson, *History of the Presbyterian Church in Kentucky*, p. 340.

and their privileges were curtailed. In Kentucky, the religious meetings of the blacks were broken up or interrupted and their Sabbath schools dispersed."[12]

When the subject of emancipation was under discussion in the Kentucky Synod one of the elders arose and stated that he owned one hundred slaves, nearly all of whom he had inherited. Many of them were so old that they could not provide for themselves, others were women and children whom no one was willing to feed and clothe for their labor. He stated emphatically that he had no desire to hold them in bondage, but that he was willing to do whatever was best for the slaves themselves. If he should free them, what would become of the aged and the women and children? Furthermore, it was a serious matter to give bond and security for the support of so many slaves of different ages and character. He could not send them out of the State, for they were intermarried with the slaves of others; and as to giving them wages, he could not, for they were eating him up as it was. With a feeling of intense interest in the slave and anxiety on his own behalf to do the right, he asked his brethren of the Synod, what he ought to do.[13] The position of this kind-hearted Kentucky slaveholder shows more clearly than any other picture we could draw the difficulties of emancipation in Kentucky even when one was convinced of the evils of the slavery system.

The final word of the Presbyterian Church on the whole subject of slavery was sounded at its General Assembly in Cincinnati in 1845, when a resolution was adopted, as submitted by Nathan L. Rice, of Kentucky, stating that it was not competent for the church to legislate where Christ and his apostles had not legislated. This, at least for the time being, proved acceptable to the churches south of the Ohio and avoided a breach in the Presbyterians such as had just taken place among the Methodists and Baptists.

The Baptists as a State organization did not pursue a policy similar to that of the Presbyterians. After the

[12] *Op. cit.*, p. 340.
[13] Blanchard and Rice, *Debate on Slavery*, p. 88.

failure of the emancipationist campaign in 1792 and again at the constitutional convention in 1799 a few members of the Baptist Church began a movement for immediate abolition under the lead of several ministers—Tarrent, Barrow, Sutton, Holmes and others. The policy which they advocated was not only one of immediate abolition but of non-fellowship with the slaveholders within their own denomination. There was no general governing body for the State, as the Baptists had several so-called associations which covered only a few counties each. The trend of opinion throughout the various commonwealth organizations was apparently against the position held by the emancipationist group, for the latter in 1807 withdrew from the regular organizations and established an association of their own which they called the Licking Locust Association. They were only able to muster the assent of twelve churches to their newer group and soon died out in importance.[14] The real sentiment of the Baptists was no doubt much like that of the Presbyterians, but these early advocates of Negro freedom in their own organization were entirely too radical even for their own church membership. Had they followed a course of action and policy more in keeping with their own constituents they might have accomplished much good, whereas, as it was, they only stirred up the feeling within their own denomination to such an extent that thereafter little progress was made towards a policy of even gradual emancipation of the slave.

Throughout the slavery era, however, the Baptists in the State were divided into the "regular" and the "separatists," the former being in favor of non-interference with the question and the latter representing the advocates of emancipation in one form or another. Both agreed that slavery was an evil, but the regular group was unwilling to make it the cause of the expulsion of a slaveholder from the church. In May, 1845, a "Southern Baptist Convention" was held at Augusta, Georgia. The meeting had been hastily called and representatives were present only from

[14] Spencer, *History of the Baptists in Kentucky*, Vol. 1, p. 186.

Maryland, South Carolina, North Carolina, Georgia, Alabama, Louisiana, Kentucky, and the District of Columbia. Mississippi, Arkansas, Tennessee and Florida were represented only by letters. The convention had been summoned as a protest against the action of the "Acting Board" of the church in the country in refusing to consent to the appointment of a slaveholder to any field of foreign missionary labors.[15] In June of the same year the Kentucky Baptists for the most part withdrew from the northern organization and pledged themselves to this newly formed southern convention. The creed was not changed. It was simply a matter of rebuke toward the northern section's attitude on the slavery question.[16]

The Methodists had also struggled to find a peaceful solution of the problem of harmonizing Christianity with slavery. At the meeting of the General Conference of the Methodist Church in 1845, several days were taken up in the debate over the status of Bishop James Osgood Andrew, of Kentucky. By inheritance and marriage he was a slaveholder. Finally he was requested by a vote of 110 to 68 "to desist from the exercise of the office of Bishop while this impediment remained." The southerners in the convention became unusually indignant, declaring that the infliction of such a stigma upon Bishop Andrew would make it impossible for them to maintain the influence of Methodism in the South.[17] So they withdrew from the convention and in May, 1845, held a convention of the Methodist churches of the Southern States in Louisville. After a nineteen-days' session they decided to set up an organization of their own to be known as the "Methodist Episcopal Church South" and to have their first meeting at Petersburg, Virginia, in May, 1846.[18]

The Kentucky Methodist Conference met at Frankfort on September 17, 1845, and the entire attention of the meeting was given over to the question of whether they would

[15] *Niles' Register*, May 24, 1845.
[16] *Ibid.*, June 28, 1845.
[17] *Ibid.*, June 8, 1844.
[18] *Ibid.*, May 17, 24, 31, 1845.

adhere to the general conference or would pledge themselves to the newly formed southern organization. Bishop Andrew appeared at Frankfort at the crucial moment and stated all the facts concerning himself and the action which the Louisville Conference had taken as a result of the trouble in the previous General Conference. By a vote of 146 to 5 they then declared that henceforth they would adhere to the Methodist Episcopal Church South, and that all proceedings, records and official acts would thereafter be in the name of the "Kentucky Conference of the Methodist Episcopal Church South."[19]

At its annual conference in 1858 held in Hopkinsville the Louisville Conference held a very heated debate over the rules of the church regarding slaveholders. Finally they voted to expunge from the General Rules the one which forbade "the buying and selling of men, women and children, with the intention to enslave them."[20] The regulation thus repealed, although it was a part of the rules of Methodism, was just another indication of the sentiment in Kentucky at that time to resent more and more the encroachments of the North on the slave system of the South and to hang on to the institution with a grim determination. But they were not willing to go to unwarrantable lengths, for at the Kentucky Conference held in Germantown in March, 1860, a proposition submitted by the sister conferences to the South with a view to further altering the rules on slavery was denied.[21]

The churches of Kentucky for the most part pursued a policy of benevolent neutrality in the struggle which the slave forces of the State were having with their neighbors to the North. The Baptists and Methodists within the commonwealth officially never made any positive contribution to the forces of either side, and they took no definite stand until the whole southern division of their general national organization withdrew from membership in the national conventions and set up an organization of their own. When

[19] *Niles' Register*, September 27, 1845.
[20] Collins, *History of Kentucky*, Vol. 1, p. 81.
[21] *Ibid.*, Vol. 1, p. 83.

this much had been done both the Methodists and Baptists of Kentucky pledged their allegiance to their respective newly formed southern conventions. On the other hand the Presbyterians of the State maintained a policy that was distinctively their own, separate and apart from any acts of their national organization. They were the only religious body in Kentucky to issue officially a constructive plan for the betterment of social and economic conditions under slavery. When it came to the advocacy of even gradual emancipation they were careful to state that the plan was only published for the benefit of the slaveholding members of their own religious body. The Presbyterians went further in their interference with the institution of slavery in the State than any other religious body, but even they were not willing to try to extend their home missionary field beyond their own membership. On the whole, the churches in Kentucky merely followed the dictates of public opinion on the subject of slavery, trying to pursue a policy of neutrality as long as possible and then when it was no longer feasible, most of them sided with the slaveholding group. The northern section of none of these religious bodies, however, was driven out of the State. There were a good many of the so-called "northern" churches which remained loyal to the old national organizations.

The summary of the actions of the three principal religious bodies of the State shows that there was a growing sentiment against the institution of slavery. Kentucky being a slaveholding State, the significance of this attitude was very important. While it may be true that the majority sentiment even among the churches was not in favor of the elimination of slavery the very fact that even a minority were coming to the front unmolested by violence and threats and favoring the gradual elimination of the established institution revealed the general trend of public opinion among the people of Kentucky. These measures were taken entirely upon their own initiative and were not prompted by an outside anti-slavery influence.

Any discussion of the evolution of public opinion in

Kentucky on the subject of emancipation and of slavery in general would be incomplete without describing the attitude of Henry Clay toward the institution in Kentucky. During almost the entire period of slavery in Kentucky he was the foremost citizen of the State and one of the principal slaveholders. From those two viewpoints alone anything that he had to say on the local type and problems of slavery is valuable in this connection.

The general position of Clay on the subject of Negro servitude has never been very widely understood. Among the radical abolitionists of the North he was looked upon as a friend of slavery for the sake of political advancement and among the slaveholders in some parts of the South he was regarded as almost a member of the Garrisonian group of the enemies of slavery. To understand Clay's real position we need only to consider his relation to the institution as it existed in his native State.

Coming from Virginia to Lexington in 1797, Clay soon found ample opportunities for a public career. He first came into prominence as a writer on slavery in the columns of the *Lexington Gazette* and the *Kentucky Reporter*. When the constitutional convention of 1799 was called for a revision of the fundamental law of the State Clay bent all his efforts towards the adoption of a system of gradual emancipation for the slaves of Kentucky. It was pointed out that there were relatively few slaves in the State and that a progressive plan of liberation would be much easier than at any future time.

The consensus of opinion at the time was that the emancipationists led by this young man from Virginia would have been successful, had it not been for the intervening excitement produced by the Alien and Sedition Laws and the resulting famous Virginia and Kentucky Resolutions of 1798. Clay threw himself heart and soul into the newer campaign against the mistakes of the Federalists and the former enthusiasm for the gradual freedom of the slaves seems to have died down in his thought as well as among the Kentucky people in general. Thus the constitutional convention of 1799 left the conditions of slavery as they were.

In a speech delivered three decades later before the Kentucky Colonization Society, Clay said in commenting on his position in 1798: "More than thirty years ago, an attempt was made, in this commonwealth, to adopt a system of gradual emancipation, similar to that which the illustrious Franklin had mainly contributed to introduce in 1780, in the state founded by the benevolent Penn. And among the facts of my life which I look back to with most satisfaction is that of my having cooperated, with other zealous and intelligent friends, to procure the establishment of that system in this state. We were overpowered by numbers, but submitted to the decision of the majority with that grace which the minority in a republic should ever yield to that decision. I have, nevertheless, never ceased, and shall never cease, to regret a decision, the effects of which have been to place us in the rear of our neighbors, who are exempt from slavery, in the state of agriculture, the progress of manufactures, the advance of improvements, and the general progress of society."[22] In his famous speech in the Senate on Abolition in 1839, referring further to his activities in 1798, Clay stated that "no one was rash enough to propose or think of immediate abolition. No one was rash enough to think of throwing loose upon the community, ignorant and unprepared, the untutored slaves of the state."[23]

Clay's private dealings with the institution were always consistent with his political principles on the subject of slavery. He bought many slaves during his lifetime but he never sold any.[24] Clay believed that the slaves should be

[22] Schurz, Carl, *Henry Clay*, Vol. 1, p. 31.

[23] Colton, *Works of Clay*, Vol. 6, p. 153.

[24] His attitude was perhaps best shown when, on a visit to Richmond, Indiana, in the fall of 1846, he was presented with a petition by a Quaker by the name of Mendenhall asking him to liberate all the slaves he owned. Clay made a rather lengthy speech to the gentleman on the general principles of the question and then came down to the practical side of the problem:

"Without any knowledge of the relation in which I stand to my slaves, or their individual condition, you, Mr. Mendenhall, and your associates, who have been active in getting up this petition, call upon me forthwith to liberate

freed, but at the same time considered the difficulties attendant upon instant emancipation. Among the mass of the slaveholders of the State, Clay was one of the very few who held a perfectly consistent attitude on gradual emancipation as was finally shown by his will.[25]

the whole of them. Now let me tell you, that some half a dozen of them, from age, decrepitude, or infirmity, are wholly unable to gain a livelihood for themselves, and are a heavy charge upon me. Do you think that I should conform to the dictates of humanity by ridding myself of that charge, and sending them forth into the world with the boon of liberty, to end a wretched existence in starvation? Another class is composed of helpless infants, with or without improvident mothers. Do you believe as a Christian, that I should perform my duty toward them by abandoning them to their fate? Then there is another class who would not accept their freedom if I would give it to them. I have for many years owned a slave that I wished would leave me, but he would not. What shall I do with that class?"

"What my treatment of my slaves is you can learn from Charles, who accompanies me on this journey, and who has traveled with me over the greater part of the United States, and in both the Canadas, and has had a thousand opportunities, if he had chosen to embrace them, to leave me. Excuse me, Mr. Mendenhall, for saying that my slaves are as well fed and clad, look as sleek and hearty, and are quite as civil and respectful in their demeanor, and as little disposed to wound the feelings of any one, as you are."

. . . .

"I shall, Mr. Mendenhall, take your petition into respectful and deliberate consideration; but before I come to a final decision, I should like to know what you and your associates are willing to do for the slaves in my possession, if I should think proper to liberate them. I own about fifty, who are probably worth about fifteen thousand dollars. To turn them loose upon society without any means of subsistence or support would be an act of cruelty. Are you willing to raise and secure the payment of fifteen thousand dollars for their benefit, if I should be induced to free them? The security of the payment of that sum would materially lessen the obstacle in the way of their emancipation."—Colton, Reed & McKinley, *Works of Henry Clay*, Vol. 6, pp. 388–390.

This sums up in Clay's own words his treatment of the slaves that were under his control. It is not to be presumed in any case that general conditions in the State were like this. There were obvious reasons why Clay couldn't get one or two of his slaves to accept freedom when he offered it, for they realized that they were far better off under his own particular care than they could ever hope to be under an absolutely free status in society.

[25] So consistent was Clay in deed as well as words in spite of all that the opposing forces had accomplished in the State of Kentucky that when he died he left a will which did for his own slaves just what he would have had others do in his lifetime. As long as he lived he refused to emancipate his slaves but when he passed away he left a written document, the following portion of which forms the eminent climax to a career of continuous labors for the eventual good of the Kentucky slave owners as well as the slaves themselves.

With a more radical policy than that of Henry Clay the Kentucky Abolition Society had been established as early as 1807, but its membership was composed largely of Presbyterian and Baptist preachers who were not in sympathy with the stand taken by the constitutional convention of 1799. It was not until about 1830 that there began in the State any real movement which was wide enough in influence to be taken as an indication of the trend of public opinion. It will be recalled that it was not until 1835 that the Presbyterian Synod was able to decide on a plan of gradual emancipation.

It was in 1831 that some 48 slaveholders of Kentucky met and declared themselves in favor of the gradual liberation of the slaves.[26] James G. Birney, who was at that time living in Danville, took this statement of the slave owners rather seriously and sent out an invitation to the prominent

"In the sale of any of my slaves, I direct that members of families shall not be separated without their consent.

"My will is, and I accordingly direct, that the issue of all my female slaves, which shall be born after the first day of January, 1850, shall be free at the respective ages, of the males at twenty-eight, and of the females at twenty-five; and that the three years next preceding their arrival at the age of freedom, they shall be entitled to their hire or wages for those years, or of the fair value of their services, to defray the expense of transporting them to one of the African colonies and of furnishing them with an outfit on their arrival there.

"And I further direct, that they be taught to read, to write, and to cipher, and that they be sent to Africa. I further will and direct, that the issue of any of the females, who are so to be entitled to their freedom, at the age of twenty-five, shall be free at their birth, and that they be bound out as apprentices to learn farming, or some useful trade, upon the condition also, of being taught to read, to write, and to cipher. And I direct also, that the age of twenty-one having been attained, they shall be sent to one of the African colonies, to raise the necessary funds for which purpose, if they shall not have previously earned them, they must be hired out for a sufficient length of time.

"I require and enjoin my executors and descendants to pay particular attention to the execution of this provision of my will. And if they should sell any of the females who or whose issue are to be free, I especially desire them to guard carefully the rights of such issue by all suitable stipulations and sanctions in the contract of sale. But I hope that it may not be necessary to sell any such persons who are to be entitled to their freedom, but that they may be retained in the possession of some of my descendants."—Colton, Reed & McKinley, Vol. 3, p. 153.

[26] Birney, William, *James G. Birney and his Times*, p. 132.

men of the State to attend an emancipation convention on December 6, 1831. After several months of determined effort Birney only succeeded in getting together nine men, all slaveholders. It is evident from the writings of Birney that he thought these men were all determined to free their slaves and that whatever plan he should propose would be accepted. But when the nine slaveholders began to talk about the existing conditions in Kentucky Birney's eyes were opened. It was pointed out that those who advocated immediate emancipation were coming more and more to be victims of social ostracism. Furthermore, Birney learned that there was among the prominent slaveholders of the State a sort of secret organization which had been formed to protect the constitutional rights of Kentucky slaveholders against the encroachments of the people from the North. James G. Birney was one of the most intelligent of the Kentuckians who favored emancipation, but the ardent enthusiasm which he had hitherto held for the future of his cause in Kentucky was decidedly cooled by this little gathering of nine slaveholders. These men showed him a point of view about which he had thought very little. Outside of the new vision which this conference gave to Birney the only result of the deliberations was that there was formed a society of slaveholders which advocated the gradual emancipation of the future offspring of slaves when they reached the age of twenty-one.[27]

Soon after this episode Birney came out in opposition to both gradual emancipation and colonization. The majority of liberal-minded Kentuckians were coming more and more to believe in these two propositions as the ultimate solution of the slave problems of the State and once Birney came out in opposition to them he was put down as a radical abolitionist. In July, 1835, the feeling of the people of Danville was aroused to the highest pitch and his anti-slavery paper *The Philanthropist* was forced to suspend publication when the local printer was bought out.[28] The

[27] Birney, William, *James G. Birney and his Times*, p. 133.

[28] *Ibid.*, p. 182. The interesting story of Birney and his troubles with his fellow townsmen does not come within the scope of this investigation and

feeling of the people throughout the State, however, was well shown by the fact that for the next two months Birney made personal visits to Lexington, Frankfort and Louisville in an attempt to get a printer to issue his newspaper. He was entirely unsuccessful and on September 13 he wrote to Gerrit Smith that he had determined to move to Cincinnati.[29] While the people of the State could not agree with Birney's attitude on slavery they were the first to admire his courage. George D. Prentice, the pro-slavery editor of the *Louisville Journal,* had this comment to make:

"He is an enthusiastic, but, in our opinion, a visionary philanthropist, whose efforts, though well intended, are likely to be of no real service to the cause of humanity. He at least shows, however, that he has the courage to reside among the people whose institutions he assails. He is not like William Lloyd Garrison living in Massachusetts, and opening the battery upon the states five hundred or one thousand miles off. He is not such a coward or fool as to think of cannonading the South from the steeple of a New England meeting house."

The climax of Birney's career in Kentucky had been reached in the early part of 1835 when he split with the Kentucky Colonization Society. Judge Underwood in the annual colonization address at Frankfort had attempted to show that the only way to exterminate slavery in the State was by African colonization. He advocated the expenditure of $140,000 annually for the transportation of four thousand Negroes between the ages of seventeen and twenty. The plan if followed for fifty years he stated would rid the State of all slaves.[30] In a letter to Gerrit Smith on January 31, 1835, Birney voiced his opposition to the plan of Judge Underwood and to any scheme of colonization. Thus on another point he was to be classed as a radical abolitionist and his career of usefulness in Kentucky was at an end. If he had chosen a more middle ground and aided

will be found treated at length in William Birney's *James G. Birney and His Times.*

[29] Birney, William, *James G. Birney and his Times,* p. 185.
[30] *Ibid.,* p. 155.

the cause of colonization, he would no doubt have accomplished much good. As it was, he was forced to leave the State after many threats and thereafter he stormed the institution of slavery in his native State from a safe region north of the Ohio River. From that time on everything that he uttered in opposition to slavery in Kentucky was met with a strong current of opposition. Where Birney might have accomplished much for his native State he really did harm because he went beyond the point where the people would listen to his advice. In September, 1834, he visited Henry Clay and that most liberal of all Kentucky slaveholders pointed out to Birney the error of his ways but the latter showed no signs of listening to advice and thereafter Clay and Birney were sworn political antagonists. Had Birney joined with Clay at this time there might have been a much brighter future in Kentucky for the cause of emancipation. As it was, Birney never receded from his position and when the Presbyterian Synod came out with its plan of gradual emancipation Birney voiced his determined opposition to the scheme because it did not favor the immediate liberation of the slaves.[31] With the advent of the abolition movement most of the Kentucky masters who were in favor of gradual emancipation receded from their position and held on firmly to the existing institution.[32]

[31] Birney, William, *James G. Birney and his Times*, p. 156.

[32] Quick to recognize this tendency, Clay referred to it in his Senate speech of February 7, 1839:

"The proposition in Kentucky for gradual emancipation did not prevail, but it was sustained by a large and respectable minority. That minority had increased, and was increasing, until the abolitionists commenced their operations. The effect has been to dissipate all prospects whatever, for the present, of any scheme of gradual or other emancipation. The people of that state have been shocked and alarmed by these abolition movements, and the number who would now favor a system even of gradual emancipation is probably less than it was in the years 1798–9. At the session of the legislature held in 1837–8 the question of calling a convention was submitted to a consideration of the people by a law passed in conformity with the Constitution of that state. Many motives existed for the passage of the law, and among them that of emancipation had its influence. When the question was passed upon by the people at their last annual election, only about one fourth of the whole voters of the state supported a call of a convention. The apprehension of the danger

The series of events from 1831 to 1835, centering around the activities of Birney, brought the attention of the public to the slavery question more than ever. As was common in all other movements of popular interest it became the custom for local gatherings to be held to discuss the problem. It was always customary at the conclusion of these meetings to draw up a series of resolutions and it is noticeable that they all voiced a similarity of sentiment on the slavery question. A typical set of resolves were those drawn up at a gathering held in Shelbyville in June, 1835:

"*Resolved*, that the system of domestic slavery as it now exists in this commonwealth, is both a moral and a political evil, and in violation of the rights of man.

"*Resolved*, as the opinion of this meeting, that the additional value which would be given to our property, and its products by the introduction of free white labor, would in itself be sufficient, under a system of gradual emancipation, to transport the whole of our colored population.

"*Resolved*, that no system of emancipation will meet with our approbation, unless colonization be inseparably connected with it, and that any scheme of emancipation which will leave the blacks within our borders, is more to be deprecated than slavery itself."[33]

These resolutions were just another indication that the sentiment of the people of Kentucky during the decade from 1830 to 1840 was in favor of gradual emancipation of the slaves and their colonization in Africa. We have seen that this was the plan of the various church bodies, and also

of abolition was the leading consideration among the people for opposing the call. But for that, but for the agitation of the question of abolition in states whose population had no right, in the opinion of the people of Kentucky, to interfere in the matter, the vote for a convention would have been much larger, if it had not been carried. . . . Prior to the agitation of this subject of abolition, there was a progressive melioration in the condition of the slaves—schools of instruction were opened by humane and religious persons. These are now all checked, and a spirit of insubordination having shown itself in some localities, traceable, it is believed, to abolition movements and exertions, the legislative authority has found it expedient to infuse fresh vigor into the police and the laws which regulate the conduct of the slaves."—Colton, Reed & McKinley, *Works of Henry Clay*, Vol. 6, pp. 153–154.

[33] *Niles' Register*, July 4, 1835.

of Kentucky's greatest statesman, Henry Clay. Added to
this we find that the majority of the liberal-minded people
of the State held to the same conviction. But why, one
asks, did all this feeling come to naught. The answer can
be better expressed in the words of a contemporary Kentuckian, Nathaniel Shaler: "From the local histories the
deliberate student will easily become convinced that if there
had been no external pressure against slavery at this time
there would still have been a progressive elimination of the
slave element from the population by emancipation on the
soil, by the sale of slaves to the planters of the Southern
States, and by their colonization in foreign parts."[34]

During the decade from 1840 to 1850 this outside pressure of which Shaler speaks was at its height. We have
seen typical examples of it within the borders of Kentucky
in the discussion of the cases of Delia Webster, Calvin Fairbank and John B. Mahan. The change in the trend of popular thought during this period does not show itself much
in the open until 1849, when the third constitutional convention was about to assemble. It was then that all phases
of the problem of slavery were discussed, in the press, in
the pulpit, on the platform and in the elections. George D.
Prentice in an editorial gave the best exposition of Kentucky
sentiment. He said: "The sentiment of Kentucky we believe to be, that slavery is an evil which must be borne with
patience, simply because there is no known plan for its
rapid extinction which would not produce incalculable sacrifices and appalling risks. At the same time we think the
people of Kentucky are not inclined to increase the evil, but
are inclined to favor its gradual emancipation and remote
termination, by prohibiting the further introduction of
slaves and by some provision tending to encourage voluntary emancipation with colonization. These measures they
believe, taken in connection with the known tendency in
widening circles to substitute free for slave labor, will hasten the social revolution in question as fast as it can be

[34] Shaler, N. S., *Kentucky*, p. 197.

carried with safety to the Commonwealth or with benefit to the colonized negro."[35]

So universal was this feeling that even Cassius M. Clay, the only real abolitionist left in the State, came out more or less in favor of it. Under his leadership there was held at Frankfort, April 25, 1849, an emancipation convention to which all the more radical element were invited. Clay himself proved to be the most radical member of the convention but when they came to draw up a series of resolutions the only ones to pass were those which favored the absolute prohibition of the importation of any more slaves into Kentucky and the complete power to enforce and perfect, under the new constitution, whenever the people desired it, a system of gradual emancipation of the slaves.[36] Here we are confronted with the unusual fact that the radical element of the State agreed with the plan of George D. Prentice, one of the chief pro-slavery men of Kentucky, and with that of Henry Clay.

While sojourning for his health in New Orleans in February, 1849, Clay sent Richard Pindell for publication a letter on the gradual emancipation of slavery in Kentucky, as the State at that time was about to hold another constitutional convention. This long and able document constitutes the most constructive program for the progressive elimination of slavery from the State that was ever drawn up. It embodied not only the fundamental principles of Clay's attitude on the Kentucky slavery question but it undoubtedly typified the real position of the average high-minded Kentucky slaveholder of that day. Clay frankly admitted that he had little hope of the immediate success of the plan, but he thought it was his duty to present the facts of the problem to the people of his own State, at a time when they were about to alter the existing constitution. The spirit of the plan as well as its context shows that Clay had thoroughly considered the emancipation question from all aspects,

[35] *Louisville Weekly Journal*, September 26, 1849.
[36] *Niles' Register*, May 9, 1849.
Clay, Cassius, *Memoirs*, pp. 175–178.
Collins, *History of Kentucky*, Vol. 1, p. 59.

especially in relation to its practical operation. The actual plan was based on three principles: (1) that any gradual emancipation should be slow in its operation, so as not to disturb the existing habits of society; (2) as an indispensable condition the liberated slaves were to be sent out of the State and colonized in Africa; (3) and the expenses of their transportation and six months subsistence were to be borne by a fund supplied by the labor of the freed negro.

Regarding the progressive plan of liberation, Clay suggested that a certain date, January 1, 1855 or 1860, be fixed for the commencement of the plan. All slaves born after that date were to be free at the age of twenty-five; but they were liable thereafter to be hired out under State authority for a period of not more than three years, in order to raise money to pay for their expenses of transportation to their colony and their subsistence for the term of six months. It was suggested that the offspring of those who were to be free at twenty-five should be free at their birth, but subject to apprenticeship until they reached their majority and then to be hired out as in the case of the parent to pay the expenses of transportation to the colony and their settlement there. In the meanwhile the master would have the usual legal rights over the slaves and could sell, devise or remove them out of the State.

Clay considered colonization to be an indispensable part of his scheme and went so far as to say that he would be "utterly opposed" to any system of emancipation without it. He firmly believed that the nearly two hundred thousand blacks along with their descendants "could never live in peace and harmony and equality with the residue of the population" if they were free. He thought the expense of colonizing should be borne by a fund from the labor of the liberated Negro because he was the individual who secured the most benefit thereby. The non-slaveholder should not be taxed for any share in the expense and the slaveholder would have enough sacrifices to make without any additional financial burdens. Clay figured that the average annual hire of each slave would be about fifty dollars, or one hundred and fifty dollars for the whole period of three years. One third of this sum would be required for the transportation of the Negro to Africa and the other two thirds would go towards a fund to establish him in his new country.[37]

The persistence of Clay in his avowed convictions on the subject of slavery and emancipation in Kentucky was kept up in spite of the fact that within a few days after the publication of his plan of emancipation throughout Kentucky the House of Representatives at Frankfort by the unanimous vote of 93 to 0 declared that "we the representatives of the people of Kentucky, are opposed to abolition or emancipation of slavery in any shape or form whatever, except as now provided by the laws and constitution of the state."[38] This was their answer to the plea set forth by Clay and strange to say the same group of men voted unanimously at the same session to return Clay for six years more to the United States Senate.

A convention of the so-called "Friends of Constitutional

[37] Clay endeavored in his plan to be fair to all parties concerned, not only the Negro but the slave owner as well, as is well evident in the following paragraph, in which he sought to show the justice of his scheme to the holders of Negroes in the State:

"That the system will be attended with some sacrifices on the part of the slaveholders, which are to be regretted, need not be denied. What great and beneficent enterprise was ever accomplished without risk and sacrifice? But these sacrifices are distant, contingent, and inconsiderable. Assuming the year 1860 for the commencement of the system, all slaves born prior to that time would remain such during their lives, and the present loss of the slaveholder would be only the difference in value of the female slave whose offspring, if she had any, born after the first day of January, 1860, should be free at the age of twenty-five or should be slaves for life. In the meantime, if the right to remove or sell the slave out of the State should be exercised, that trifling loss would not be incurred. The slaveholder, after the commencement of the system, would lose the difference between the value of the slaves for life and slaves until the age of twenty-five years. He might also incur some inconsiderable expense in rearing from their birth the issue of those who were to be free at twenty-five, until they were old enough to be apprenticed out; but as it is probable that they would be most generally bound to him, he would receive some indemnity from their services until they attained their majority."

[38] Collins, *History of Kentucky*, Vol. 1, p. 58.

Reform" had been held at the State capital on February 5, 1849, and had drawn up a series of twelve resolutions on the several questions which were to be debated in the constitutional convention. They made mention incidentally of the desired reforms in connection with slavery stating "that we do not desire or contemplate any change in the relative condition of master and slave in the new Constitution, and intend a firm and decided resistance to any such change. We have no objection to a proper provision for colonizing the present free blacks, and those who shall hereafter be set free, but protest against abolition or emancipation without the consent of the owner, unless upon full compensation and colonization."[39]

This element dominated the convention. The body not only ignored any plan of emancipation but drew the reins of the existing institution tighter than ever before by incorporating in the Bill of Rights the famous phrase that "the right of property is before and higher than any constitutional sanction, and the right of the owner of a slave to such slave and its increase is the same and as inviolable as the right of the owner of any property whatsoever." Such a statement was, however, not brought on by the words of Clay, but was a direct answer to the "higher law than the constitution" plea of the abolitionists.[40] The convention amended the standard article on slavery with a section to the effect that the "General Assembly should pass laws

[39] *Niles' Register*, February 21, 1849.

[40] We know how Clay felt about this matter, for he referred to it at length in his speech in the Senate on February 20, 1850, in the debate on the Compromise resolutions. Speaking particularly of his letter of emancipation he declared: "I knew at the moment that I wrote that letter in New Orleans, as well as I know at this moment, that a majority of the people of Kentucky would not adopt my scheme, or probably any project whatever of gradual emancipation. Perfectly well did I know it; but I was anxious that, if any of my posterity, or any human being who comes after me, should have occasion to look into my sentiments, and ascertain what they were on this great institution of slavery, to put them on record then; and ineffectual as I saw the project would be, I felt it was a duty which I owed to myself, to truth, to my country, and to my God, to record my sentiments. The State of Kentucky has decided as I anticipated she would do. I regret it; but I acquiesce in her decision."—Colton, Reed & McKinley, *Works of Henry Clay*, Vol. 3, p. 353.

providing that any free negro or mulatto immigrating to, and any slave thereafter emancipated in, and refusing to leave that State, should be deemed guilty of a felony, punished by confinement in the penitentiary.''

The obvious purpose of this amendment was to reduce the number of Negroes in the State. Accordingly every slave emancipated was forced to leave the State and the Negro population was decreased just so much every time any slaves were set free. The convention was thus willing to do something towards eliminating the Negro, but was not in favor of any scheme of a general gradual liberation of the slaves. The necessary legislative act for carrying out the provision of the constitution was enacted March 24, 1851.[41] This law only went half way in that it only prevented those Negroes who had been freed in Kentucky from living in the State. It was not until March 3, 1860, that the prohibition was extended to all free Negro immigration into the State.[42] An interesting development of this policy was shown in the enactment of the legislature in 1863 which declared it unlawful for any Negro or mulatto claiming to be free under the Emancipation Proclamation to migrate to or remain in the State. Any Negro violating this law was to be treated as a runaway slave.[43]

The desire of the State authorities to eliminate the free Negro was accompanied by constructive measures in behalf of the emancipated slave. On March 3, 1856, the State legislature passed a law appropriating $5,000 annually to aid the Kentucky Colonization Society in the transportation of free Negroes to Liberia.[44] The universal sentiment of the time was that the salvation of the Negro race rested in their elimination from the State even as free men and their transportation to their native African soil. Henry Clay of all others was the most persistent advocate of colonization.

We have seen that the general trend of public opinion from about 1798 had been progressively in favor of gradual

[41] Collins, *History of Kentucky*, Vol. 1, p. 61.
[42] *Ibid.*, Vol. 1, p. 83.
[43] Session Laws of 1863, p. 366.
[44] *Ibid.*, 1856, Vol. 1, p. 50.

emancipation provided it was coupled with some form of colonization which would remove the liberated Negroes from the State. Public sentiment, however, received a serious set-back about 1838 with the beginning of the Underground Railroad system and the incoming of the abolitionist literature. In a speech in the Kentucky legislature of 1838 James T. Morehead, one of the leading anti-slavery statesmen of the State, portrayed the coming of the newer era in the history of Kentucky slavery when the people would make more strenuous efforts to hold firmly to the slavery institution. Morehead pictured the popular mind in these words: "Any man who desires to see slavery abolished—any friend of emancipation, gradual or immediate—who supposes for a moment that now is the time to carry out this favorite policy, must be blind to the prognostics that lower from every quarter of the political sky. Sir, the present is not the period to unmanacle the slave in this or any other state of the Union. Four years ago you might have had some hope. But the wild spirit of fanaticism has done much to retard the work of emancipation and to rivet the fetters of slavery in Kentucky. . . . The advocates of abolition—the phrenzied fanatics of the North, neither sleep nor slumber. Their footsteps are even now to be seen wherever mischief can be perpetrated—and it may be that while the people of Kentucky are reposing in the confidence of fancied security, the tocsin of rebellion may resound through the land—the firebrand of the incendiary may wrap their dwellings in flames—their towns and cities may become heaps of ashes before their eyes and their minds drawn off from all thoughts of reforming the government to consider the means necessary for their self-preservation—the protection of their families and all that is dear to men."[45]

Such was the idea of one of the most prominent public men of Kentucky and such became in time the opinion of the average citizen who had come to believe in gradual emancipation as the hope and solution of the Negro problem in the State. The future course of events regarding slavery in

[45] *Maysville Eagle*, April 11, 1838.

Kentucky is to be explained by this radical change of mind. Thus did the wise and constructive plans of the gradual emancipationists come to naught with the incoming of the radical abolitionist movement which the Kentucky populace thought would bring about a civil insurrection among the slaves in their own State. The abolitionists misunderstood the gradual emancipation movement in Kentucky and really fanned the flame of the pro-slavery sentiment that came in its place.

BIBLIOGRAPHY

Laws

Littell's Laws, 5 volumes, 1792–1819.
Session Laws, 70 volumes, 1792–1863.
Revised Statutes:
1. Wickliffe, Turner and Nicholas, 1 volume, 1852.
2. Stanton, 2 volumes, 1860.
3. Myer's Supplement, 1 volume, 1866.

Law Digests

Littell and Swigert, 2 volumes, 1792–1822.
Pirtle, 2 volumes, 1832.
Loughborough, 1 volume, 1842.
Morehead and Brown, 2 volumes, 1792–1834.
Monroe and Harlan, 2 volumes, 1852–1853.
Frye, Poindexter and Smith, 1792–1852.
Cofer, 1853–1867.

Reports

Hughes' Reports, 1 volume, 1785–1801.
Sneed's Reports, 1 volume, 1801–1805.
Hardin's Reports, 1 volume, 1805–1808.
Bibb's Reports, 4 volumes, 1808–1817.
A. K. Marshall's Reports, 2 volumes, 1817–1821.
Littell's Reports, 5 volumes, 1822–1824.
T. B. Monroe's Reports, 7 volumes, 1824–1828.
J. J. Marshall's Reports, 7 volumes, 1829–1832.
Dana's Reports, 9 volumes, 1833–1840.
Ben Monroe's Reports, 18 volumes, 1840–1857.
Metcalfe's Reports, 4 volumes, 1858–1863.
Duvall's Reports, 2 volumes, 1863–1866.

Other Documents

House Journals, 61 volumes, 1793–1863.
Senate Journals, 58 volumes, 1801–1863.
Collected Documents (State Departments), 1839–1863.
American Anti-slavery Society Reports.
Niles' Register, 1811–1849.

Newspapers

(The dates give the extent of the existing files)
American Antiquarian Society
   Bardstown Candid Review, 1807–1810.

Bardstown Western American, 1803–1804.
Bardstown Repository, 1814–1816.
Frankfort American Republic, 1810–1812.
Frankfort Argus of Western America, 1808–1819.
Frankfort Commentator, 1818–1819.
Frankfort Guardian of Freedom, 1798–1804.
Frankfort Palladium, 1798–1816.
Lexington American Statesman, 1811–1813.
Lexington Independent Gazetteer, 1803–1804.
Lexington Kentucky Gazette, 1794–1819.
Lexington Reporter, 1808–1820.
Lexington Stewart's Kentucky Herald, 1801.
Lexington Western Monitor, 1815–1817.
Louisville Correspondent, 1814–1817.
Louisville Gazette, 1807–1809.
Louisville Public Advertiser, 1824–1830.
Louisville Western American, 1806.
Louisville Western Courier, 1814–1815.
Maysville Eagle, 1815–1817.
Richmond Globe, 1810.
Richmond Luminary, 1812–1816.
Russellville Mirror, 1806–1809.
Washington Union, 1814–1817.
Washington Weekly Messenger, 1803.
Winchester Advertiser, 1814–1815.
Winchester Kentucky Advertiser, 1815–1817.

Lexington (Ky.) Public Library
Frankfort American Republic, 1810–1812.
Frankfort Argus of Western America, 1824–1830.
Frankfort Commonwealth, 1838–1839.
Lexington Kentucky Gazette, 1787–1865 (remarkable file).
Lexington Reporter, 1808–1832.
Lexington Observer and Reporter, 1832–1865.
Lexington Kentucky Statesman, 1849–1865.
Lexington Inquirer, 1844–1849.
Lexington Intelligencer, 1834–1839.
Lexington Public Advertiser, 1820.
Lexington Western Monitor, 1818–1819.

Kentucky State Library
Bardstown Herald, 1852–1855.
Carroll Courier, 1851.
Carroll County Times, 1855–1856.
Democratic Banner, 1852.
Georgetown Herald, 1851.
Kentucky Age, 1856–1857.
Kentucky New Era, 1853–1864.
Kentucky Tribune, 1852–1857.
Lebanon Post, 1853–1857.

Bibliography

Lexington Observer and Reporter, 1845–1851.
Owensboro Gazette, 1853–1854.
Shelby News, 1852–1857.
Maysville Eagle, 1857–1858.
University of Chicago (Durrett Collection)
Frankfort American Republic, 1810–1811.
Frankfort Argus of Western America, 1816–1830.
Frankfort Commentator, 1823–1832.
Frankfort Commonwealth, 1832–1862 (scattering issues).
Frankfort Guardian of Freedom, 1799–1805.
Frankfort Kentuckian, 1828–1831.
Frankfort Kentuckian and Commentator, 1832.
Frankfort Palladium, 1798.
Lexington Kentucky Gazette, 1794–1836 (scattering issues).
Lexington Reporter, 1810–1817.
Lexington Kentucky Reporter, 1817–1827.
Lexington Western Luminary, 1824–1835.
Lexington Western Monitor, 1814–1820.
Louisville Public Advertiser (semi-weekly), 1819–1829.
Louisville Public Advertiser (daily), 1830–1841.
Louisville Daily Courier, 1857–1860.
Louisville Daily Democrat, 1862–1865.
Louisville Focus (weekly), 1828–1829.
Louisville Focus (daily), 1831.
Louisville Herald (daily), 1832–1834.
Louisville Presbyterian Herald, 1846–1862.
Maysville Eagle (weekly), 1846–1847.
Maysville Eagle (semi-weekly), 1835–1845.
Maysville Eagle (tri-weekly), 1845–1858.
Maysville Herald (tri-weekly), 1847–1848.
Maysville Herald (daily), 1848–1849.

Kentucky: General Works

Allen, William B. A History of Kentucky. Louisville. 1872.
Allen, James Lane. The Blue Grass Region of Kentucky. New York. 1911.
Arthur, Timothy S., and Carpenter, W. H. The History of Kentucky. Philadelphia. 1850.
Bishop, Robert H. Outline of the History of the Church in Kentucky. Lexington. 1824.
Butler, Mann. A History of the Commonwealth of Kentucky. Louisville 1824.
Collins, Lewis and R. H. History of Kentucky. 2 volumes. Covington (Ky.). 1874.
Cook, J. F. Old Kentucky. New York. 1908.
Cotterill, R. S. History of Pioneer Kentucky. Cincinnati. 1917.
Davidson, R. History of the Presbyterian Church in Kentucky. New York. 1847.

Filson, John. The Discovery, Settlement and Present State of Kentucky. Wilmington. 1784.
Filson Club Publications
    Brown, John Mason. The Political Beginnings of Kentucky. 1889.
    Durrett, Reuben T. John Filson. 1884.
    Durrett, Reuben T. The Centenary of Kentucky. 1892.
    Durrett, Reuben T. The Centenary of Louisville. 1893.
    Martin, Asa Earl. The Anti-slavery Movement in Kentucky. 1918.
    Perrin, William Henry. The Pioneer Press in Kentucky. 1888.
    Price, Samuel W. The Old Masters of the Blue Grass. 1902.
    Speed, Thomas. The Political Club, Danville, Ky. 1894.
    Whitsitt, William H. Life and Times of Judge Caleb Wallace. 1888.
Ford, S. H. History of the Kentucky Baptists. (A series of articles in the Christian Repository. 1856–1858.)
Gray, John Thompson. A Kentucky Chronicle. New York. 1906.
Johnson, E. Polk. History of Kentucky and Kentuckians. 3 volumes. New York. 1912.
McElroy, Robert M. Kentucky in the Nation's History. New York, 1909.
Marshall, Humphrey. The History of Kentucky (second edition 2 vols.). Frankfort. 1824.
Perrin, William H., and Battle, J. H., and Kniffin, G. C. Kentucky: a History of the State. Louisville. 1886.
Redford, A. H. History of Methodism in Kentucky. 3 volumes. Nashville. 1868.
Shaler, Nathaniel S. Kentucky: a Pioneer Commonwealth. Boston. 1885.
Smith, Zachary F. The History of Kentucky. Louisville. 1886.
Speed, James. The Union Cause in Kentucky (1860–1865). New York. 1907.
Spencer, John J. History of the Baptists in Kentucky. 2 volumes. Cincinnati. 1880.
Townsend, J. Kentuckians in History and Literature. New York. 1907.
Vance, W. R. Slavery in Kentucky. (Washington and Lee University thesis.) 1896.
Watts, William C. Chronicles of a Kentucky Settlement. New York. 1897.
Webb, B. J. Centenary of Catholicity in Kentucky. Louisville. 1884.

KENTUCKY: LOCAL AND COUNTY HISTORIES

Anon. History of Union County. Evansville. 1886.
Battle, J. A., and Perrin, W. H. Counties of Todd and Christian: Historical and Biographical. Louisville. 1884.
Boyd, Lucinda. Chronicles of Cynthiana and other Chronicles. Cincinnati. 1894.
Boyd, Lucinda. The History of the City of Winchester and the County of Clark. (MSS. in the Durrett Collection.)
Casseday, Benjamin. The History of Louisville. Louisville. 1852.
Chenault, William. The Early History of Madison County. (MSS. in the Durrett Collection.)
Deering, Richard. Louisville, Her Commercial, Manufacturing and Social Advantages—including Her History. Louisville. 1859.
Duncan, Samuel M. Early History of Jessamine County. Nicholasville. 1876.

Bibliography

Finley, Alexander C. The History of Russellville. Russellville. 1878.
Johnson, Frank. History of Franklin County. Frankfort. 1912.
Johnson, J. Stoddard. Memorial History of Louisville. Chicago. 1896.
Jones, Mary K. History of Campbell County. 1876.
Maccabe, Julius P. B. Directory of the City of Lexington and of the county of Fayette for 1838 and 1839—containing an epitomized history of the city and its present condition. Lexington. 1838.
McMurtie, H. Sketches of Louisville and its Environs. Louisville. 1819.
Perrin, William H. Counties of Christian and Trigg: Historical and Biographical. Chicago. 1884.
Perrin, William H. History of Bourbon, Scott, Harrison and Nicholas Counties. Chicago. 1882.
Perrin, William H. History of Fayette County. Chicago. 1882.
Ranck, George W. History of Lexington, Kentucky. Cincinnati. 1872.
Reid, Richard. Historical Sketches of Montgomery County. Mt. Sterling. 1882.
Rothert, C. A. History of Muhlenburg County. Louisville. 1913.
Starling, Edmund L. History of Henderson County. Henderson. 1887.
Young, Bennett H. A History of Jessamine County. Louisville. 1898.

Valuable Contemporary Pamphlets

Address to the Non-slaveholders of Kentucky—read at Louisville, April 10, 1849. Louisville. 1849.
Address to the People of Kentucky on the Subject of Emancipation. 1849.
Address to the People of the United States with the Proclamation and Resolutions of the Pro-slavery Convention at Lexington. St. Louis. 1855.
Address to the Presbyterians of Kentucky, proposing a plan for instruction and emancipation of their slaves—by a committee of the Synod of Kentucky. Newburyport. 1836.
Blanchard, J., and Rice, David. Debate on Slavery. Cincinnati. 1846.
Duncan, James. Treatise on Slavery. Vevay, Ind. 1824.
Fee, John G. An Anti-slavery Manual. New York. 1851.
Fee, John G. Non-fellowship with Slaveholders, the Duty of Christians. New York. 1852.
Metcalfe, Samuel L. A Collection of Some of the Most Interesting Narratives. Lexington. 1821.
Rice, David. A Kentucky Protest against Slavery. 1792.
Stevenson, Thomas B. Report to the Convention of Southern Methodist Ministers—held at Louisville in the summer of 1845. Louisville. 1845.
Webster, Delia A. Kentucky Jurisprudence. History of the Trial of Miss Delia A. Webster on a charge of aiding slaves to escape. Vergennes, Vt. 1845.

Contemporary Writings

Allbach, James. Annals of the West. Pittsburgh. 1857.
Barre, W. L. Speeches and Writings of Thomas F. Marshall. Cincinnati. 1858.
Bowen, E. Slavery in the Methodist Episcopal Church. Auburn. 1859.
Buckingham, James Silk. The Eastern and Western States of America. 3 volumes. London. 1842.

Clarke, Lewis and Milton. Narratives of the Sufferings of Lewis and Milton Clarke during a captivity of more than twenty years among the slaveholders of Kentucky. (A violent anti-slavery publication.) Boston. 1846.
Clay, Cassius M. Life Writings and Speeches. Cincinnati. 1886.
De Bow, J. D. B. Statistical View of the United States. Washington. 1854.
Fairbank, Calvin. How the Way was Prepared. Chicago. 1890.
Fearon, H. W. Sketches of America. London. 1818.
Flint, James. Letters from America. Edinburgh. 1822.
Flint, Timothy. Geography and History of the Western States. 2 volumes. Cincinnati. 1828.
Flint, Timothy. Recollections of the Mississippi Valley. Boston. 1826.
Greeley, Horace. Writings, Speeches and Addresses of Cassius Clay. New York. 1848.
Kendall, Amos. Autobiography of Amos Kendall. Boston. 1872.
Littell, William. Political Transactions in and Concerning Kentucky. Frankfort. 1806.
Melish, John. Geographical Description of the United States. Philadelphia. 1822.
Michaux, F. A. Travels to the West of the Allegheny Mountains. London. 1805.
Palmer, John. Journal of Travels in the United States. London. 1818.
Paxton, J. D. Letters on Slavery. Lexington. 1833.
Pickard, Kate E. R. The Kidnapped and the Ransomed. (Anti-slavery publication.) New York. 1856.
Robertson, George. George Robertson's Scrap Book. Lexington. 1855.
Robertson, George. Life of George Robertson. Lexington. 1876.
Shaler, Nathaniel S. Autobiography. Boston. 1909.
Weld, Isaac. Travels in America. 2 volumes. London. 1799.
Weld, T. D. American Slavery As It Is. New York. 1839.
Winterbotham, William. An Historical, Geographical, Commercial and Topographical View of the United States. 4 volumes. London. 1799.

General Secondary Works

Ballagh, James Curtis. A History of Slavery in Virginia. Baltimore. 1902.
Birney, William. James G. Birney and His Times. New York. 1890.
Brackett, Jeffrey R. The Negro in Maryland. Baltimore. 1889.
Buckley, J. M. History of Methodism in the United States. 2 volumes. New York. 1898.
Calhoun, Arthur Wallace. Social History of the American Family. 3 volumes. Cleveland. 1917–1918.
Chaddock, R. E. Ohio Before 1850. New York. 1908.
Cobb, Thomas R. R. An Inquiry Into the Law of Negro Slavery. Philadelphia. 1858.
Coleman, Mrs. Chapman. Life of John J. Crittenden. 2 volumes. Philadelphia. 1871.
Collins, W. H. Domestic Slave Trade of the Southern States. New York. 1904.

Bibliography

Colton, Calvin. Reed, Thomas B.; and McKinley, William. Works of Henry Clay. 7 volumes. New York. 1896.
Helper, Hinton Rowan. The Impending Crisis of the South. New York. 1860.
Hurd, John Codman. The Law of Freedom and Bondage in the United States. 2 volumes. New York. 1858–1862.
Little, Lucius P. Ben Hardin—His Times and Contemporaries. Louisville. 1887.
Rogers, Joseph M. The True Henry Clay. Philadelphia. 1904.
Schurz, Carl. Life of Henry Clay. 2 volumes. Boston. 1887.
Smith, William Henry. A Political History of Slavery. 2 volumes. New York. 1903.
Stroud, G. W. Sketch of the Laws Relating to Slavery in the Several States of the United States. Philadelphia. 1856.
Trexler, Harrison Anthony. Slavery in Missouri (1804–1865). Baltimore. 1914.
Weston, G. M. The Progress of Slavery in the United States. Washington. 1857.
Wheeler, Jacob D. The Law of Slavery. (A compilation of decisions of the Federal and State courts.) New York. 1837.
Wilson, Henry. History of the Rise and Fall of the Slave Power in America. 2 volumes. Boston. 1874.
Woodson, Carter G. The Education of the Negro Prior to 1861. New York. 1915.